ASPERGER SYNDROME

Maxine Rosaler

The Rosen Publishing Group, Inc.
New York

For my son

Published in 2004 by The Rosen Publishing Group, Inc.
29 East 21st Street, New York, NY 10010

Library of Congress Cataloging-in-Publication Data

Rosaler, Maxine.
Coping with Asperger syndrome/by Maxine Rosaler.
    p. cm.—(Coping)
Summary: Presents information about Asperger's syndrome, including theories concerning its cause, its various characteristics, and management of the condition.
Includes bibliographical references and index.
ISBN 0-8239-4482-4 (lib. bdg.)
1. Asperger's syndrome—Juvenile literature. [1. Asperger's syndrome. 2. Autism.] I. Title. II. Series.
RC553.A88R67 2004
616.89'82—dc21

                                     2003007046

Manufactured in the United States of America

Contents

Introduction

Most of us wouldn't have to look much further than ourselves to find behaviors that might seem a bit odd. For example, many of us are always forgetting to do things like turn off the lights or lock the door behind us when we leave the house, and if that description doesn't fit us, we all know plenty of people whom it would fit. And we all know people who worry about things that don't seem worth worrying about and people who seem to be in worlds of their own, oblivious to what is going on around them. We all know people who, for one reason or another, keep to themselves and people who always seem to be saying or doing the wrong thing without even realizing it. We also all know people who cannot stand crowds or noise, people who are irrationally stubborn, and people who always seem to be getting upset about one thing or another. We all know people who talk incessantly, unaware of the fact that others are not interested in listening to what they are saying.

Taken separately, none of these oddities necessarily means that there is anything clinically wrong with a person. It might simply mean that the person is quirky or a little peculiar. But put these characteristics together in a single individual, amplify and distort them, and you might have a person with Asperger syndrome (AS).

In the United States, Asperger syndrome has only been recently diagnosed. It is categorized as an autistic spectrum disorder. The autistic spectrum includes a group of disorders that range from classical autism to Asperger. Although Asperger was discovered in 1944, it wasn't until the 1980s that most doctors had ever even heard of it. After that, it took more than a decade before doctors were familiar enough with the condition to start diagnosing their patients with it.

Since it is relatively "new" and has such an unusual assortment of symptoms, scientists have not yet decided what the exact definition of Asperger should be. Although scientists have not yet been able to come up with an official definition of Asperger that everyone can agree on, they do agree on a few things about it.

Asperger syndrome is a neurobiological disorder. This means that it is a disorder that results from abnormalities in the brain. Every area of the brain is responsible for performing a certain function, and the neurobiological abnormalities that are present in Asperger affect areas of the brain that are responsible for a person's ability to function as a social being in the world.

Asperger syndrome is what is known as a developmental disability. A developmental disability is a disability that a person is born with, and it is a condition that will most likely affect that person in one way or another throughout the course of his or her life.

Scientists agree that people with Asperger syndrome usually share the following set of characteristics, although the degree to which they exhibit these characteristics can vary greatly from person to person.

↝ They have significant difficulties interacting with other people.

↝ They are often unusually or irrationally stubborn.

↝ They often have unusual interests that they pursue with an inordinate amount of intensity.

↝ They either overreact or underreact to things affecting the senses.

↝ They tend to think in concrete and literal terms and have difficulty understanding nuances and double meanings.

↝ They have a marked lack of common sense.

Asperger mostly affects males—estimates are that there are four to nine times as many males as females who have Asperger. People with Asperger sometimes have trouble paying attention and are often very hyper, so much so that they are often mistakenly diagnosed with attention deficit hyperactivity disorder (ADHD). They also tend to be very clumsy and can have terrible handwriting. But, as with everything else with Asperger, there are many exceptions. For example, there are some people with Asperger who are accomplished calligraphers.

Letters always fascinated Billy. When he was a baby, he would stare for hours at the mobile of the alphabet that hung above his crib. Whenever his mother took him out in his stroller, he would spell out the signs on the store awnings they passed. He would read the logos on the shirts and jackets of everyone he saw. He always seemed to be much more interested in the logos than he was in the people who were wearing them. By the time he was two years old, Billy had taught himself how to read.

Billy's parents were delighted with how smart their son was, but there were also some things about him that worried them. For one thing, Billy did not seem to feel pain. When he was four years old, his mother noticed a burn on his arm that was well on its way to healing. It was a third-degree burn—the most painful kind—but Billy never said anything about it. He never cried when he fell down and hurt himself. But if an eyelash got stuck in his eye or if his mother tried to clip his toenails or wash his hair, he would cry out in anguish. Billy also seemed to be unaware of danger— he would walk into traffic without even looking, and he was always trying to climb out the window of the family's sixth-floor apartment.

Yet there were many things that terrified Billy. The sight of a dog walking down the street would cause him to tremble with fear. He was so afraid of the stuffed zebra his grandparents had given him for his birthday that his mother had to throw it down the garbage chute.

He would also get upset about the oddest things—if he heard about a building being torn down in his neighborhood, nothing short of the reassurance that it would be rebuilt tomorrow would calm him down. He would be devastated if one of his TV shows was moved from one time slot to another. And the decision to take a different route to his grandmother's house could set off a major temper tantrum.

One day the principal of his nursery school called his mother in for a meeting. The principal told her that Billy never played with the other children, that he was always hiding in the closet, and that he was always turning the light switches on and off no matter how many times he was told not to do so. She said that she had never seen a child quite like Billy.

When children have problems like this, she explained, the board of education could test them to find out what was wrong. The law required the board of education to do this testing free of charge, and if they found anything wrong with the child, they were required to do what they could to fix the problem.

When she got home, Billy's mother told her husband about what the principal had said. Billy's father was furious. He said that there was nothing wrong with his son. He reminded her how Billy's mind was always so full of questions and ideas. "Why is it dark in outer space?" "Does the universe end?" "Why does clay dry up?" Every day he was grappling with big issues, big ideas, things that were way beyond the grasp of other children. Billy's father told Billy's mother that he could not imagine or hope for a child who was more wonderful or gifted than Billy.

Finally, when Billy was nine, his mother decided that she couldn't wait any longer to get Billy tested. The psychologist who was testing Billy let his mother sit in. Whenever Billy refused to answer a question, his mother would tell her that it was because he was stubborn. But the psychologist told her that it wasn't because Billy was stubborn. "It's neurological," she said. There was a problem with Billy's brain. He had Asperger syndrome, she explained. Children with Asperger, she said, had the same kinds of problems with communication and socialization that autistic children did, but their deficits were not nearly as severe. She said they could be taught how to overcome many of their problems and that children with Asperger were usually smart.

Billy's mother felt an ache in her throat that was so painful she could barely speak. The psychologist patted her on the arm and told her that she shouldn't worry about Billy. Children with Asperger had a good chance of growing up to lead very productive lives, she said, and the fact that they were intelligent helped a lot. She told her that it was a good thing that she had brought Billy in to be evaluated when he was still young. He had plenty of time to learn what he needed to know in order to get along in the world, but she said that they had better get started right away because the longer they waited, the harder it would be for Billy to learn.

Billy's mother couldn't hold back her tears. The psychologist put her hand on her shoulder and told her again that she shouldn't worry. She told her that Billy *might not grow up to be president of the United States and that he would probably never be the life of the party, but that there was a good chance that he would grow up to live a full and productive life. He could get married and have a family and career. She even mentioned the names of some very famous, very successful people who were thought to have Asperger. Billy's mother tried to calm down, and she started to gear herself up for the long struggle that lay ahead.*

As this story indicates, Asperger syndrome is a unique diagnosis. The people it affects often have exceptional abilities. Yet, the realities of everyday life that are simple for most people can be very challenging and complicated for them.

Learning to Recognize
Asperger Syndrome

People with Asperger syndrome look like other people. They can do most of the things that other people can do, some even noticeably better. They usually have remarkable memories and are often very good at activities that require logical thinking, like doing puzzles or working with computers.

Most people with Asperger are intelligent, sometimes very intelligent, and sometimes even brilliant. At school, they often excel in most of their subjects, especially math, science, and music. In addition to being good students, they're usually well behaved. They wouldn't go out of their way to be mean or nasty. They wouldn't bully another child or pick on anyone. They wouldn't be purposely disruptive or cheat on an exam. They're usually very careful, often painstakingly so, about following all the rules.

A Hidden Disability

The weaknesses that people with Asperger syndrome have are often not apparent, at least not at first. Yet these weaknesses are so profound that they affect the lives of people with AS in ways that would be difficult for most people to imagine. The things that people with Asperger have trouble doing, the things that in some cases they simply cannot do, are the things that most people without Asperger take for granted.

I remember that when I first found out that my son had an autistic spectrum disorder I was completely devastated. But then when he was later diagnosed with Asperger syndrome, I felt relieved since the person who diagnosed him told me that he wouldn't have any problems learning, that he was very smart, and that all his problems would have to do with how he functioned socially. I remember thinking, "Big deal. He won't be social." My husband and I have always been very awkward socially and prefer to be alone most of the time. But I have since learned that having social problems means a lot more than not being the most popular kid in the school.

"Mental Colorblindness"

While people with Asperger syndrome can be quite intelligent, when it comes to understanding other people—their thoughts, their feelings, what pleases them, what displeases them—they are often at a complete loss. Dr. Michael D. Powers, a psychologist who has written extensively about Asperger syndrome, compares the disorder to "mental colorblindness." Powers explains, "A person who is colorblind has nearly normal vision and can cope quite well, except in certain situations where color identification is essential—like traffic lights."[1]

"Social Dyslexia"

Dr. Richard Howlin, of the Chelsea Center for Learning Disorders in Chelsea, Michigan, says that Asperger is a kind of "social dyslexia." He says that just as otherwise intelligent children with dyslexia have trouble learning to read the printed word, children with Asperger syndrome have trouble learning to understand other people. "As the dyslexic child struggles with the alien world of print, so too does the Asperger child find himself lost in reading social interactions and intent. In both stories, a naturally unfolding developmental process is stunted. The child is often helpless, if left without the support and understanding of the adult world."[2]

Trouble with Nonverbal Communication

Dr. Simon Baron-Cohen, a research psychologist who has written extensively about Asperger syndrome, says that people with AS are "mindblind," meaning that they are not capable of "reading" other people. In other words, they are not able to guess what people's intentions are based on what are known as social cues or nonverbal communication. Gestures, facial expressions, the tone of a person's voice, and body language all fall under the category of nonverbal communication.

More than 65 percent of all communication is nonverbal. In fact, most of the signals people send each other don't come from words at all. A furrowed forehead, a lifted eyebrow, a raised hand, or a sharp edge to the voice can often do a better job of communicating how a person thinks and feels about something than any number of words ever could.

Most people are able to understand what a person is thinking or feeling based on the nonverbal signals he or she sends out alone. There are actually parts of our brains that are specifically designed to pick up the nonverbal signals that people send each other all the time. For reasons that no one yet understands, the parts of the brain that are supposed to do this work do not function properly in people who have Asperger syndrome. Jerry Newport, a person with AS who frequently lectures about it, says that for people with Asperger, it is as if all the social signals people send each other were being sent to them in a foreign language. "Imagine if all those signals came to you in Cantonese, and you spoke only English," he says. "That's what having Asperger is like."[3]

It is very difficult for people with AS to understand what other people are thinking or feeling or what their intentions might be. Since they don't understand or even pay attention to things like a person's tone of voice or facial expression, they may completely miss the fact that something someone said was intended to be a joke or was meant to be ironic.

People with AS can also often appear to be emotionally detached from other people, though, in reality, they may not be emotionally detached at all.

Discomfort in Social Situations

This lack of awareness about how other people think and feel often makes people with Asperger syndrome very uncomfortable in social situations. Something as simple as saying "hello" to someone they run into on the street can be a major ordeal for them.

For reasons that no one has yet been able to figure out, people with AS cannot pick up on the rules of social interaction that are second nature to most people. Most people without Asperger, for example, know that they should look at people when they are talking to them. They also know that they should occasionally give people a signal that they are interested in what they have to say—a smile, a nod, a comment of some kind. A person with AS doesn't know to do simple things like this, and as a consequence, he or she will often behave very awkwardly, often saying or doing something that is socially unacceptable without even realizing it.

Inappropriate Behavior

People with Asperger do not realize that there are certain things that are socially inappropriate to say to other people. As a consequence, they might end up saying things that are embarrassing to themselves or others—things that are even outrageous.

For example, if a person with AS sees someone who is overweight, not only might he think nothing of saying that the person is "fat," but he will very likely bombard the person with a series of questions about his weight. He might ask how much he weighs, what size pants he wears, how large his waist is, how much food he consumes in the course of a day, what his blood pressure is, and so on.

Heightened Sensitivity

In addition to finding the social aspects of daily life to be totally bewildering, people with AS often have problems with their nervous systems. The nervous system regulates how people's senses respond to the environment. As a result of nervous system irregularities, people with AS often tend to be overly sensitive, or hypersensitive, to sound, sight, taste, smell, and touch. Some have hearing that is so acute that the sound of the doorbell can feel like a sharp needle piercing their eardrums. Thunder can sound like a bomb exploding.

The reverse of this can also be true—people with Asperger can be hyposensitive, or have senses that are blunted or dulled. A person who is hyposensitive might not feel pain or cold. For example, sweltering temperatures that would send most people in search of the nearest air-conditioned room might feel perfectly comfortable to a person who is hyposensitive.

In addition to being easily distracted by things that are happening around them, people with AS often get distracted by their own thoughts. Students with AS can get so absorbed in what they are thinking about that they will tune out everything the teacher is saying. People with Asperger also often have what is known as auditory processing problems, which means they have trouble making sense of what they hear. Spoken language can sound like noise to them.

His hearing is so acute that the sound of an airplane flying overhead always makes Freddy scream out in pain. He can hear the phone ringing when no one else can. He can't bear the sound of the vacuum cleaner; it affects him so strongly that the sound of it will reverberate in his ears long after it has been turned off. His other senses, too, are unusually acute.

On a warm day, he will tell his mother to close the windows of their apartment because the smell of dog urine on the sidewalk five stories below bothers him. He can't bear fluorescent lighting; he says that the flickering of the filaments upsets him.

Need for Sameness

Since so much of their world is difficult for them to understand and interpret, people with AS don't want the things they know to be true and constant to be open to interpretation. They often have a very strong desire for everything to be the same. The closing down of a familiar store in the neighborhood or the cancellation of a class can cause great distress to someone with AS.

Will, a fourteen-year-old with AS, has such a need for sameness that he gets very upset whenever he hears of anything being called by a name that is different from the one that it had originally been given. When his father told him that the name of the West Side Highway in New York City had been changed to the Joe DiMaggio Highway, tears welled up in his eyes and he demanded that the highway's original name be officially restored immediately.

Allan always wanted everything to be the same. He was so attached to sameness that when the seasons changed from winter to spring, he would refuse to change out of his winter clothes. He would insist on wearing his jacket, hat, scarf, and gloves, even though to do so would make him sweat profusely. Change of any kind upset him. Once, when he was five, his mother rearranged the furniture in the living room. Allan got so upset about it that his mother felt she had no choice but to put everything back exactly where it used to be, down to the flower vase that she had moved from the cocktail table to the top of the bookcase.

Peculiar Obsessions

People with Asperger also tend to be very obsessive. They have a desperate, inexplicable need to do certain things in a certain way all the time. For example, a person with AS might feel compelled to touch a light switch every time he passes one, or he might insist on using the same dishes and silverware every day. A person with AS might insist on wearing the same clothes for months on end, and every time she walks down the street she might insist on walking on the curb, skipping over every crack in the cement.

Every day when Eli came home from school, he would go straight for his school's directory of names and addresses, open it up, and stare at it for as long as his mother would let him. It would always be a struggle for his mother to tear him away from the directory to come into the kitchen to do his homework.

"Everything he does like that is so overboard and so nonstop to the point of driving me nuts," his mother says. However, she adds, she has learned that Eli's odd behaviors are often not as useless as they might at first appear to be. She says that Eli memorized all the information about the kids in his school that was listed in the directory, and he now knows the birthday

of everyone in his school. His mother says, "That's good, because it helps him be more socially connected. So it can be useful."

Special Interests

People with Asperger also have a marked tendency to develop special interests, which they explore with an unusual amount of intensity and passion. Sometimes the interests they pursue are very odd. Taking apart doorknobs, saving the little stickers that come attached to apples and bananas, collecting cashier receipts, and learning everything there is to know about RV trailers are examples of unusual interests. The often highly idiosyncratic nature of the AS person's special interests is one of the hallmarks of the disorder.

However, the interests of children with AS are not always necessarily unusual. Math, science, history, geography, and reading (many people with AS are able to read at a very early age) are examples of typical AS interests. Weather, astronomy, and various types of machinery are other subjects that people with Asperger are typically interested in. Maps are a particular favorite. Dr. Hans Asperger, the psychiatrist who discovered this condition in 1944, noted in the paper he wrote about the syndrome that children with the disorder appeared to be fascinated with modes of transportation. In his paper, he wrote about children who memorized the tram lines in Vienna, Austria, down to the last stop.

Michael always loved playing with words. When he was three, he changed the first line of the song "Oh

Susanna" to "I come from Alabama with a Band-Aid on my knee," replacing "banjo" with "Band-Aid." When he was four, he said that if a person dove off a diving board into a pool that didn't have any water in it, then the diving board should be called a "dying board." Once he asked for "mental floss," and when his father asked him what he wanted to do with a thing like that, he said, "To clean my head." His parents were always so delighted with how clever their son was. It never occurred to them that Michael's precocious use of language might be a sign that there was something wrong with his brain.

A Target for Ridicule

Sometimes a child's special interests can make him a target for ridicule. One ten-year-old boy who was obsessed with viruses and bacteria was nicknamed Virus Boy by his classmates.

The potential for ridicule becomes more of a problem the older a child is and the more unusual his special interests are. An eighteen-year-old who talks incessantly about pickup trucks could be viewed as eccentric, but an eighteen-year-old who is obsessed with electric stoves and gas ranges would be considered to be rather weird.

Barbara Oxenfeldt, the parent of a child with Asperger, reports that there seems to be a certain pattern to the way her child pursues his special interests. "His interest grows and grows and grows until it peaks," says Oxenfeldt. "It will reach a certain point where it's just insufferable, and then it ends. It seems to have a certain momentum."[4]

When David was small enough to be carried around on his parents' backs, his favorite thing to do was ride the subway. Before he was two years old, he had memorized all the stops on the line that ran in his neighborhood—he would always call out the stops before the conductor made the announcement that the train was about to pull into a station. The other passengers would smile at him and say what a cute little boy he was.

When David was three years old, he noticed a subway map that his father had left lying open on the coffee table in the living room. He went over to examine it and was instantly mesmerized by it. He loved following all the lines of all the different stops from one end to the other. Thus began David's life-long fascination with maps.

David started collecting subway maps of New York City when he was five. When he was seven, he started collecting maps of subways and buses in cities across the United States. Eventually, he was collecting maps of bus and subway systems in cities around the world.

David was very particular about which maps he collected. He knew which manufacturers made good quality United States maps and which manufacturers made good quality foreign maps, and he would only collect maps that had been made by the manufacturers he liked.

David recently turned fourteen. He now likes to create his own maps of countries that he invents. Studying bus and subway maps is still his greatest passion.

Diagnosing Asperger

There is no official test that can diagnose Asperger syndrome. Doctors arrive at a diagnosis by deciding whether the person appears to fit a set of symptoms that are listed in the *Diagnostic and Statistical Manual of Mental Disorders*, the reference book that catalogs all the psychiatric disorders that are officially recognized by the American Psychiatric Association. Asperger syndrome wasn't included as a disorder until the fourth edition of the manual was published in 1994.

Deciding whether a person should be diagnosed with Asperger syndrome is up to the individual judgment of the doctor doing the diagnosis. The accuracy of each diagnosis will therefore depend very much on the doctor's skill and experience. Sometimes it just boils down to the doctor's intuition about whether the person seems to fit the profile of someone with Asperger. Dr. Raun Melmed, a developmental pediatrician with an expertise in autism and Asperger, says that one of the cardinal features of Asperger is extreme individuality. "Everyone and his or her grandmother thinks they step to the beat of a different drummer," he says. "But these are individuals who really do."[5]

Since the symptoms of AS overlap with those of many other similar disorders, people with AS are often misdiagnosed with other conditions. ADHD, obsessive-compulsive disorder (OCD), nonverbal learning disability (NLD), and various types of emotional disorders are the conditions that people with AS are most commonly misdiagnosed with.

Comorbid Disorders

Children with AS often have other disorders. When a person with a disability has another disability, the other disability is known as a comorbid disorder. Dr. Melmed says that it is more common for children with AS to have other conditions than it is for them not to have comorbid disorders. "In Asperger, comorbidity with other disorders is the rule rather than the exception," says Dr. Melmed.[6]

Dr. Melmed also says that if Asperger is the only diagnosis the child is given, then the person doing the diagnosing is likely missing something.

Letting Children Know

Parents often ask when they should tell their children that they have a diagnosis of Asperger syndrome. Dr. Brenda Smith Myles, an assistant professor of special education at the University of Kansas who has written a number of books about Asperger, says that the sooner parents tell children about their diagnosis, the better off most of them will be. "The more any of us know about ourselves, the better off we are. However, this is a decision that must be made on a child-by-child basis," she says.

Knowing about his diagnosis gives a child the ability to better deal with it himself. If he understands why he has a problem doing something, he will be able to address that problem and seek possible solutions for it. For example, if a child is having trouble following directions in class, he will know it is because he has an auditory processing disorder. Knowing this, he will be able to ask his teacher to write the instructions down for him so that he can understand them. "When that happens, that's when we have a success story," says Dr. Myles.[7]

Often, children have reported that in the long run learning that they had Asperger has helped them do a better job of coping with their difficulties. Adam Shery, a teenager with AS, says that being teased about having Asperger was a lot harder for him before he found out about his diagnosis. "My quirkiness was perceived as a weakness, and I was called a weakling," he says. "Understanding why I behaved the way I did helped me accept myself better. I knew it wasn't because I was weak but because I had a neurological disorder."[8]

Most people agree that when parents tell their children about the diagnosis, they have to be careful about not making the children feel bad about it. Children with AS need to have it explained to them in terms of what their strengths and weaknesses are—they need to be told that there are always some things that people are good at doing and other things that they are not so good at doing. It needs to be made clear to them that they have nothing to be ashamed about. They need to be told that while they might be different from other people, they are not defective.

Diet, Vitamins, and Medication

Since Asperger is a biological disorder, it makes sense to treat it biologically. Diet, vitamins, and medication are the treatments that are most commonly used to address the problems of brain chemistry that occur with Asperger. All these treatments have varying levels of success.

What works for one child will not necessarily work for another, and parents often have to do a lot of experimenting before they can find an approach that will work for their child.

Some parents say that changing their child's diet helps alleviate some of the symptoms of AS. Other parents report that giving their children vitamin and mineral supplements has been very helpful. Drug therapy is the approach that is most commonly used, and it seems to be the one that is most effective in treating symptoms.

All drugs have side effects, some serious and some not so serious. Also, many of the medications that are used to treat children with psychiatric disorders have not been specifically tested on children. For these and other reasons, parents are often reluctant to give drugs to their children.

"Parents think that if they medicate their children, they are going to be poisoning them or turning them into zombies," says Dr. Steven Wolf, a pediatric neurologist. "No doctor wants to turn your child into a zombie. A good doctor will work with a family until he gets the right medication or the right combination of medications that works best for your child."[9]

There are no medications that can "cure" Asperger, but there are several that can help alleviate some of the symptoms, such as problems with attention, hyperactivity, obsessiveness, compulsiveness, temper tantrums, and impulsive behavior. The effectiveness of the medication will vary very much from child to child. After weighing all the alternatives, most parents decide that if there is a drug that could help alleviate some of their child's symptoms and suffering, they have no choice but to try it.

The following are the kinds of medications that are used most often to treat the symptoms of AS.

➣ **Antidepressants** These can help alleviate anxiety or depression as well as obsessive and compulsive behaviors. Antidepressants like selective serotonin reuptake inhibitors (SSRIs) are used most commonly for AS.

➣ **Stimulants and amphetamines** These are used to treat the symptoms of ADHD and can sometimes help improve concentration and reduce hyperactivity in children with AS.

➣ **Neuroleptics** These drugs, which are usually used to treat psychotic conditions such as schizophrenia, are thought to be useful for treating the explosive or unpredictable behaviors often associated with AS.

What Is
Asperger Syndrome?

Most people would be surprised to realize how many decisions go into doing simple everyday things like crossing the street or answering the phone or buying a piece of pizza at the local pizza parlor. These are tasks that people typically do without even thinking. When most people cross the street, for example, they know to look both ways for cars. When they pick up the phone, they say "hello" and have a conversation. When they go to the pizza parlor, they know that if there is a line of people in front of them at the counter, they will have to wait their turn.

But the fact is that for all these simple, everyday actions, there are dozens of decisions and choices that a person has to make, decisions he or she is not even aware of making. In addition, there is always the chance that something unexpected will occur, and a person must be prepared to make decisions about what to do about these unexpected events as well.

For example, when someone is about to cross the street, if an old woman who is walking beside him trips, he will be faced with the decision about what to do. Most likely he will have the common sense, and the courtesy, to offer to help. When someone answers the phone and the person on the other end says that he will win a million dollars if he just sends in a check for a hundred dollars, he will most likely know that the person on the other end is trying to play a trick. When someone gets a slice of pizza and it turns out to be cold, he will know enough to ask the person behind the counter to heat it up.

But everyday decisions like these and hundreds of others like them present great challenges to people with Asperger syndrome. Buying a slice of pizza at the local pizza parlor can, in its way, be as complicated for a person with Asperger as doing a problem in advanced calculus would be for most people.

A Different Type of Learning

When doctors try to explain what it is that makes a person with Asperger different from a so-called normal, or neurotypical, person, they point to the fact that interacting with other people is not something that comes naturally to people with Asperger. The simplest, most basic forms of social interactions are often very difficult for them.

People with Asperger syndrome are not influenced by their social experiences in the same way that neurotypical people are. From the time they are children until the day they die, most people are always picking up things from their environment that teach them something about other people. This process of osmosis—gradual, often unconscious learning from the environment—is how most people acquire information about how to get along in the world.

But what comes naturally to most people does not come naturally to people with Asperger syndrome. Children with

Asperger do not learn about other people through osmosis. They have to be taught the things that neurotypical people pick up unconsciously.

The Autistic Spectrum

As mentioned before, the scientists who study the mind and its problems call Asperger syndrome an autistic spectrum disorder. Before we can begin to understand what the term "autistic spectrum" means, we need to understand what autism is.

Autism is a mental disorder that has been known about since the 1940s. Until as recently as the 1980s, it was thought to be a single condition, one that was completely disabling. When people thought of autism, they pictured someone who was completely withdrawn and had no interest at all in other people, someone who would perform strange repetitive motions like rocking back and forth or flapping his arms. Most people usually thought of a person with autism as being incapable of speech.

There are autistic people who fit this description. Around 70 percent of classically autistic people are mentally retarded, and 50 percent can't speak. However, these people constitute only one part of the autistic spectrum.

What Is a Spectrum?

Just as a light spectrum refers to all the variations of shades and tones that exist within the color range, the autistic spectrum refers to the wide range of variations that can exist within the diagnosis of autism. Think of all the different shades and variations there are for the color blue, from the powder blue of a baby's blanket to the darkness of the ocean. Autism, too, can come in variations of such striking differences that it is hard to believe that it is all the same basic condition.

As Dr. Raun Melmed says, "There is a big spectrum of human differences and a very wide palette of colors. Individuals with autism are made up of many different colors. And individuals with Asperger are made up of many different colors, too."[1]

At the lower end of the autistic spectrum are people who appear to be completely unconnected to other people. These people constitute what is called the low-functioning end of the spectrum. This includes people who cannot speak at all and people who are mentally retarded.

At the other end of the spectrum—the so-called high-functioning end—are people who have high IQs, good thinking skills, and very large vocabularies. The symptoms of these people can be so mild that it is difficult to detect that there is anything clinically wrong with them at all.

Although the symptoms of Asperger syndrome are much less disabling than the low-functioning forms of autism, the two disorders have a number of the same symptoms, including difficulties with socialization, communication, and behavior. The fact that the two diagnoses have so many symptoms in common is the reason that Asperger is thought to be an autistic spectrum disorder.

Asperger Versus Autism

If people with Asperger and people with severe autism share so many of the same basic characteristics, what then is the difference between the two disorders? This is a question that scientists have been grappling with since Asperger

Extremes of Behavior

Most people with AS want to have contact with other people, but since they lack social skills and social instincts, they do not know how to go about it. This inability to understand how to get along with other people can express itself in a range of different ways.

On one extreme are people who want to have little to do with other people—they might withdraw into themselves, engage in solitary pursuits, or appear to be loners. On the other extreme are those who desperately want to make contact and will forge ahead and try whatever occurs to them, no matter how inappropriate. They might intrude on other people's conversations or invade other people's personal space, hugging friends and strangers alike.

became a separate diagnosis in 1994. To complicate this question, there is another diagnosis called high functioning autism (HFA), which refers to those people who have the least disabling forms of autism.

Scientists have not yet decided whether HFA and Asperger are the same or altogether different disorders. Dr. Uta Frith, a well-known expert on autism, says that people with Asperger syndrome have "a dash of autism."[2]

Dr. Lorna Wing, the person who introduced Asperger syndrome to the English-speaking world, says that giving

Asperger a definition distinct from autism "is at best a work in progress."[3] Some people refer to Asperger syndrome as "high IQ autism."

Eventually, the label of Asperger might disappear altogether and be replaced with a term like "high-functioning autistic spectrum disorder." In the meantime, almost everyone agrees that Asperger is a form of autism, and when discussing the disorder, scientists and doctors usually group people with the diagnoses of HFA and AS in one category.

People with AS say that being aware of their symptoms helps them develop strategies for coping with their disability. "Essentially it's good for me to be aware of my AS because it helps me control how I act," says Adam Shery. Adam says that when he started caring about what other people thought of him, he started to understand that how he acted would affect how he was perceived. He realized, for example, that when he called out in class, his classmates would look down on him for it. "I feel guilty about the way I had been acting before in that I totally embarrassed myself," he says. "I could assume that now, whereas before I didn't really give any thought to it."

Adam says that since he started caring about what other people thought of him, his social instincts have developed in many ways. He says that he now knows how to read social cues. For example, if a person he is talking to starts talking to someone else, he can tell that that person is not interested in what he has to say, whereas before he would just go on talking. He also says that he is not as obsessive as he used to be. He recalls how when he was younger he used to throw a fit if he couldn't watch his favorite TV shows. "Learning how ridiculous it is to behave like that has helped me to control it," he says.

Making eye contact was another problem that Adam has made a lot of progress with. He says that he decided to start making eye contact with people when he realized that people thought that he was not looking them in the eye because he was being dishonest. He says that made him feel very nervous. "I was wondering whether people were questioning the value of what I was saying, whether they were questioning the truth of it," he says.

A Label Doesn't Define a Person

Although scientists devote a lot of time to determining whether Asperger is autism, they are always quick to warn against placing too much importance on the label, whatever it is. Nearly all professionals agree that a label cannot begin to summarize who a person is. "All human beings have unique combinations of strengths and weaknesses," Dr. Melmed explains. "The strongest of us in some areas are often, at the same time, the weakest in others. When individuals exhibit multiple weaknesses in related areas of life, they are often labeled. However, these labels mustn't set limits on the human spirit."[4]

The fact that people with AS are usually very different from each other, with no two people sharing the exact same set of symptoms, is another reason why it would be wrong to attach too much importance to the label. Dr. Brenda Myles says that every time she's about to go into a room to work with a child, she takes a deep breath and says to herself that she hopes she will be able to understand that child. "It is important to understand the characteristics associated with Asperger syndrome, but it is much more important to understand the child," she says. "We're just beginning to understand these kids."[5]

No matter what the diagnosis is, it all ultimately comes down to what the child's individual strengths and weaknesses are and what needs to be done to help build on those strengths and deal with those weaknesses. Rather than concerning themselves with the diagnosis, the people who are responsible for helping children with Asperger should focus on understanding each child in terms of his or her unique needs.

Dr. Jed Baker, a psychologist with an expertise in Asperger, says that people working with children with AS need to ask themselves a number of questions before they begin working with a child. Some of those questions include the following.

- ➾ Is this a child who has difficulty with social skills, and if so, which ones?

- ➾ Does the child know what to do and why he should do it?

- ➾ If he does know what to do, what's keeping him from doing it? Is it because his impulsiveness is getting in the way?

↩ Does the child want to connect with other people but is not able to because he does not know how?

↩ Is the child obsessed with intrusive thoughts, and if so, could that be the reason he seems to be distracted?

↩ Is the child distracted, impulsive, and hyperactive all the time?

↩ Are there certain circumstances that seem to set him off?

"These are just a few of the important questions that need to be asked in order to determine what course of treatment to pursue," says Dr. Baker. "Deciding whether someone has the Asperger or high functioning autism diagnosis does not yet have important treatment implications."[6]

The Different Stages of Asperger

Asperger syndrome is thought to be a lifelong disability. This means that people with AS will most likely show signs of having the condition throughout the course of their lives. This is not to say that the symptoms will not change—they do change considerably, even though the overall problems do not usually go away.

Each year can bring new achievements, new struggles, and new opportunities for growth. Usually children get better and learn. Although they are not likely to completely outgrow their AS, what they can do is get better at pretending to be like other kids.

"Perhaps the most significant aspect of . . . children with Asperger syndrome is how hopeful the prognosis can be," writes Dr. Michael D. Powers in his book *Asperger Syndrome and Your Child: A Parent's Guide.* "With understanding and down-to-earth strategies for helping these children cope with their condition, their futures can be bright indeed." But, he cautions, success will be possible only if the children are taught how to use their strengths to compensate for their weaknesses. "If your child can do these things, with your help, he may accomplish great things."[1]

One of the biggest obstacles that stands in the way of a child's chances for success is the tendency of special educators to regard the AS child solely in terms of his or her disability. "What I've noticed is that people with a background in special education tend to read pathology into so many behaviors," says Helene Lesser, the mother of a fourteen-year-old with AS. "This is the big danger—seeing everything your kid does as being something pathological. It can be so destructive. You really have to keep yourself from doing that, and it isn't helped by teachers or principals who tend to do that all the time. I can see from my own experience of reading this stuff that the more you read, the more you see pathology. Seeing the pathology doesn't always make you more sympathetic—sometimes it just makes you want to stop it."[2]

If the educator considers the child's strengths, she will likely discover a wealth of resources that she can put to valuable use. For example, a teacher could find a way of taking the child's special interest and incorporating it into a lesson or she could ask him to share his interest with the class. If the child is gifted in math, the teacher can have him tutor a classmate who has trouble with math.

A child with AS needs to be carefully educated—point by point, step by step—about people and about the aspects of daily living that a neurotypically developed person picks up without even knowing. There is a lot of hard work that is required of the parents, the teachers, the therapists, and most of all, the student. But if everyone does what is best for the child, the results will be more than worth it.

As the mother of an eleven-year-old with Asperger says, "If we all do our jobs well, in the end we will have a person who at least resembles a 'normal' human being. The seams might show, but we will have a person who can function independently within the society at large."[3]

Most experts agree that in order for the children to have the chance to grow up to lead full and productive lives, it is essential that they be given the right kind of treatment and education as early as possible. In an interview in the *Boston Herald*, Dr. Powers said, "I tell parents that if an adult with AS is not gainfully employed, somebody messed up."[4]

The Preschool Years

During the early years, the greatest challenges for people with AS is to learn the basic social skills—simple practical skills like learning that she has to respond when spoken to, that she has to look people in the eye, and that she has to refrain from doing things that will disturb or anger other people. The AS preschooler is unlikely to show much interest in other children, or if she is interested in playing with them, she will only want to do so on her terms—she will have to be the one who dictates what game they will play, and she will be the one who will determine the rules of the game.

Sensory Issues

If a child with AS has sensory issues, it is during these early years that they will present the most difficulty. This is the time when children with Asperger are likely to try to calm down their disordered nervous systems by doing things like spinning around in circles way past the point that would make most people very dizzy, burrowing themselves under the cushions of the couch, or hiding in closets in an effort to shut out the sensations that are so overwhelming to them. During early childhood, a child with AS may be terrified by the sound of the vacuum cleaner or find sunlight to be unbearable and painful to his or her eyes.

There are different schools of thought on how a child can cope with sensory difficulties. Occupational therapists think that the best way of dealing with sensory problems is to find physical ways to calm down the child. A person who follows a discipline of psychology known as behaviorism would think that the child would have to learn how to cope with sensory issues. The behaviorist's approach would be to direct the child's attention away from the source of discomfort and get him or her to focus on something positive and constructive, something that would be socially appropriate.

Obsessive Behavior

The obsessive behaviors that are so typical of people with Asperger will begin at this time—a child who is obsessed with order, as many children with Asperger tend to be, might insist on arranging his toys in a certain way. For example, he might line up all of his stuffed animals according to species or color.

During these early years, the child will seem to be irrationally stubborn about doing things in a certain way, such as taking the same route to the park every day, insisting on eating from a particular plate, or sitting on a particular chair. During these early years, any disruption in routines and rituals will likely result in the child having major temper tantrums.

There are different opinions about how to deal with obsessive behaviors. One approach is to try to diminish or eliminate these behaviors by rewarding the child for restraining himself from being obsessive and by punishing him for indulging in these behaviors. Eventually, indulging in the behavior would no longer be a source of pleasure and not indulging in the behavior would be rewarding. Another approach is for the child to indulge in the behavior in certain places, for a certain number of times, or during certain periods of the day.

Special Interests

The child's special interests also begin to emerge during these early years. Letters, numbers, and shapes are a common source of fascination for children with Asperger during their preschool years. At this age, a child might memorize the license plate numbers of all the cars in his neighborhood. Or he might be able to recite entire scripts of his favorite videos, which he will insist on watching over and over again.

Special skills and talents may also show up at this age. It's not unusual to find a three-year-old who knows the difference between a trapezoid and a parallelogram, a four-year-old who could give detailed directions on how to get from New York to Boston, or a five-year-old who knows the capital of every state in the United States, along with its major industries.

Language Deficits

While problems with language are usually not as apparent during these early years, certain aspects of the child's language might stand out. The vocabularies of many children with Asperger tend to be very advanced—it is not unusual for a five-year-old with Asperger to have the vocabulary of a fourteen-year-old, yet that same child might be incapable of having a simple conversation.

Many children with AS also develop a very odd, stilted way of speaking, with little variation in intonation or phrasing. As the child gets older, his language deficits and his difficulties understanding the rules of appropriate social behavior often become more apparent. During the middle school years, his social problems will be greater than at any other time during his school years.

Adolescence

Adolescence is difficult for everyone, and it can be particularly difficult for a child with Asperger. The problems of adolescence can be further complicated for those children who have the milder forms of Asperger, since it is often during the middle school years that the disorder is likely to be first diagnosed. To learn that there is something that makes the child different can be devastating during this stage of development when everyone wants so desperately to be like everyone else. Middle school is also the time when children are least tolerant of children who are different from themselves.

Social Exclusion
During the middle school years, children are often asked to do a lot of group work; teachers will often leave it up to

the children to pick each other to work together on group projects and the child with Asperger is often the last one to be picked, if he or she is picked at all. In a post he wrote for an Asperger Web site, a student with AS warned against leaving it up to the children to choose their own groups for group activities.

Bullies

Children who delight in preying on the weak and vulnerable are at the peak of their performance during middle school. At no other time are bullies able to exercise more power or inflict more pain than during the vulnerable years of adolescence. Not only will the "strange" child with Asperger be an easy target for the bully, but he might be so naive that he might not even realize that he is being bullied.

One thing that bullies like to do is to take advantage of people or try to make them do something that is silly, stupid, or wrong. The AS child's naïveté will put him in greater danger of falling into the bully's traps. Teachers must put a stop to bullying as soon as they see it happening. They should also deal with the issue of bullying and teasing by teaching children to be more tolerant of people who are different from themselves. Other children also have to understand what they can do to help a child with a disability.

One way of making children more tolerant of children with AS is to educate them about the condition. Lori Shery, the mother of a sixteen-year-old with Asperger and the founder of the Asperger Syndrome Education Network (ASPEN), says that she wishes people today were as aware of Asperger syndrome as they are of ADHD. "When

ADHD was a new diagnosis, people would say 'Oh my gosh,'" she says. "Now everyone has it. No one is afraid of it. I'd like to make Asperger a household name like ADHD is today, so that people will understand it and not be afraid of it."[5]

Depression and Isolation

In addition to having to deal with being persecuted and shunned by their peers, children with Asperger usually become more aware of how different they are from the other children during middle school. This awareness can create a lot of anxiety. They might become very unhappy and depressed about their situation, and they might express their unhappiness by having temper outbursts or by withdrawing more into themselves.

Many children cope with their depression through therapy, which can help them find practical solutions to their problems. When looking for a therapist to help their child, parents sometimes use someone who has experience treating children with AS. "You have to be with enough children with Asperger to understand their confusion about the world and to know where the gaps are and what you can do to fill them in," says Dr. Norma Doft, a clinical psychologist who specializes in working with children with Asperger syndrome.[6]

Traditional therapy that tries to explore the emotions is of no use to children with AS since the world of the emotions is so confusing to them to begin with. "If you try to get them to have insights into their own emotions in a traditional sense, you're going to be wasting your time," says Dr. Elizabeth Roberts, a neuropsychologist who specializes in treating children with AS. "The therapy has to be tangible, concrete, and very real."[7]

Often, however, the depression can get so bad and so debilitating that more aggressive measures are necessary. In this case, parents often have no choice but to put their children on antidepressant medications. Drug therapy has proven to help many children.

Social Deficits

Social life and social behavior become much more complex and much more demanding during adolescence. As the social demands become more complex, the child's social deficits will become an even greater handicap. For example, children with Asperger might not be able to pick up on social cues enough to know whether someone wants to be their friend. A student whom no one likes and whom everyone thinks is weird might not know enough about how the social hierarchy works to realize that the most popular girl in the class would probably not want to go out with him. He would also not understand that there might be some other girl, one who is less popular and perhaps a little bit more like him, who would like to go out with him.

High School

By high school, children are usually more tolerant of individual differences. If the student does well academically, this might give him the opportunity to gain respect from the other students. If he is lucky, he may be able to form friendships based on the interests he shares with some of his fellow students. If the AS student is interested in things like computers, math, or science, joining clubs that center around these interests would be a good way for him to make friends with other young people who share his interests.

College

During college, students tend to be even more tolerant of differences and idiosyncrasies. Also, there is a lot more opportunity to be independent during this time, both socially and academically. During college, students do a lot of work on their own. They can often work at their own pace. And since there are more opportunities to take courses that interest them, students with AS have the chance to pursue their special interests within the context of their college course work.

The Workplace

Fitting in with the ebb and flow of the daily routine of going to work can be very stressful and demanding. "It all comes down to finding the right job to fit the right person," says Dr. Powers. He also says it is wise for the person with Asperger to avoid work situations that involve a lot of social contact and instead to seek situations where he can be left to work on his own. He adds that the key to success in work is to find a niche that can make use of the person's special talents.[8]

The Future

The overwhelming worry of every parent of a child with Asperger syndrome is whether the child will be able to live an independent life. Since AS has been recognized by doctors only recently, there have been no studies to show what becomes of children with AS who have been taught in childhood how to cope with their difficulties. However, there is a general consensus among professionals that if children are given the chance to acquire the skills and knowledge that they need in order to survive in the adult world, there is hope that they will one day be able to find a place for themselves in the world.

Common Misconceptions

Up until a few years ago, hardly anyone in the United States had even heard of Asperger syndrome. Recently, however, Asperger has been in the news a lot. This, on the whole, has been a good thing, since physicians now know to be on the lookout for signs of the disorder and more educators are familiar with it. On the other hand, all this media attention has also led to the creation of certain myths about Asperger that are not altogether true.

Nicknames

Asperger syndrome has become such a popular subject in the press lately that it is sometimes referred to by nicknames like geek syndrome or nerd syndrome. It is most commonly referred to as the little professor syndrome, since children with the disorder can be very intelligent and have a tendency to talk incessantly about their special areas of interest.

In addition to being insulting, nicknames like nerd syndrome and geek syndrome can be misleading, since they imply that people with Asperger syndrome are merely eccentric or odd. A nickname like little professor syndrome is misleading as well, since it implies that everyone who has AS is brilliant. While it is true that there are a number of people with AS who are brilliant, half of the people with this disorder have average IQs.

Common Misconceptions Among Professionals

Professionals charged with the responsibility of treating people with Asperger have a good deal of difficulty understanding the disorder as well. One mistake professionals often make is jumping to the conclusion that if a person has Asperger, he must have *all* the characteristics that are associated with it.

Seeing the person as a collection of symptoms—symptoms that he may or may not have—does him great injustice. It can result in severely underestimating the person's abilities and denying him the opportunity to learn how to do what he is capable of doing.

The following are some other common misconceptions about people with Asperger syndrome.

➯ *People with Asperger syndrome prefer to be alone and don't want to have friends.*

While it is true that many people with Asperger syndrome do like to be alone, this doesn't mean that they don't want to have friends. What is more often the case is that people with AS want to fit in socially and have friends, but they don't know how to go about it.

49

➭ *People with Asperger don't care about other people.*

People with Asperger have trouble understanding what other people are thinking and feeling, but that doesn't mean they don't care about other people—they do, but they just don't understand them. Just as you wouldn't say a person who can't carry a tune would be indifferent to the beauty of music, you can't say that a person with Asperger is indifferent to other people.

➭ *Children with Asperger lack the ability to get emotionally attached to other people.*

Many children with Asperger (and autism) are very attached to their parents and to other members of their extended families. With time, patience, and education, they can also learn how to form emotional bonds with other people.

➭ *Everyone with Asperger has very restricted interests that are limited to rote learning and lead nowhere.*

While it is true that many people with Asperger have interests that seem to be very limited in value and scope, many have a variety of interests, some of which have the potential of leading to meaningful careers. Even people with seemingly meaningless interests can be taught how to develop their interests into something that is productive and useful.

↪ *People with AS can't appreciate humor.*

This is one of the biggest misconceptions about people with Asperger. People with AS are often very witty. Many are particularly fond of wordplay and are especially adept at making puns and coming up with concepts and ideas that have absurd, ironic twists.

↪ *Everyone with Asperger syndrome takes things very literally.*

While being literal is a feature of the disorder, not everyone with Asperger interprets everything literally.

Since AS has only recently been identified as a disorder, there are no statistics on what can be accomplished with children who have been given help when they are still young enough for it to do them the greatest good. But everyone who works with children with AS agrees that you don't need a research study to tell you that limits should never be set on what the future may hold for these children. There is no telling how far they can go.

However, in order to get to that future of fulfilled promise and potential, children with Asperger need a huge amount of support, and not just from the professionals who have been trained to work with them. Children with AS need help from the people they come into contact with every day. Their parents, neighbors, and peers have a vital role to play in their lives.

Learning how to function as a member of society is not easy for anyone, and most of us never stop trying to learn how to do a better job of it. Children with AS have to try to do a better job of it as well. For them, the process of learning and growing just happens to be a lot harder, and there are a lot more obstacles. But if everyone pitches in and does what they can to help, the chances are that children with AS will eventually learn what they need to know to get along in the world. And they will be able to grow up to fulfill their potential—whatever that may be—which in some cases could be to make some very important contributions to a world that in many ways can be so very difficult for them to live in.

Asperger Syndrome Throughout History

Although it wasn't until 1994 that most U.S. doctors even realized that Asperger syndrome existed, it is a condition that has been around throughout human history. Uta Frith writes in her book *Autism: Explaining the Enigma* about Brother Juniper, a Franciscan monk from the Middle Ages who seems to have had many of the hallmark symptoms of Asperger—the literal-mindedness, the naïveté, the extreme impracticality. Dr. Frith says that Brother Juniper so literally interpreted the rules of charity and poverty of his order that he was always giving away the clothes off his back.

Dr. Frith uses the example of the famously indifferent and famously logical detective Sherlock Holmes to illustrate the attachment to logic that is so characteristic of people with Asperger. Since emotions are so confusing to them, people with AS often rely on logic to make sense of the world. As a consequence, it often seems that people with AS are more attached to logic than they are to people.

Dr. Frith points out that "autistic intelligence" is very different from what our idea of intelligence usually is. She describes it as being "the opposite of conventional learning and worldly-wise cunning." She says that in certain ways Sherlock Holmes could be said to exemplify the unique and very distinctive kind of intelligence that people with Asperger and high functioning autism often possess. She characterizes the Sherlock Holmes kind of autistic intelligence as being "absent-mindedness in relation to other people, but single-mindedness in relation to special ideas."[1]

Many of the hallmark symptoms of Asperger are qualities that are often associated with genius. Scientists and journalists alike enjoy speculating about famous people who might have or might have had AS.

Albert Einstein is an example that is often cited. Einstein's trademark sloppiness and absentmindedness are said to be signs that the famous physicist might have had Asperger.

A Brief History of Asperger Theories

The symptoms and behaviors that make doctors decide that a child has an autistic spectrum disorder were first described in 1943 in the United States by Dr. Leo Kanner and in 1944 in Austria by Dr. Hans Asperger. Kanner and Asperger were unaware of each other's work, and it was a great coincidence that they both made the same discovery at the same time.

As a group, the children Asperger and Kanner described shared many of the same basic features. Both Kanner and Asperger were struck by the children's lack of a natural connection to other people. They both used the word "autistic" to describe them—"autistic" means solitary.

There were also some significant differences between the children Kanner described and the children Asperger described. The children described in Asperger's scientific paper were less disabled, and for the most part they had average or above average intelligence. Because of these differences, the disorder that Asperger identified was eventually given the name Asperger syndrome. The children Kanner identified are usually thought to have classic autism.

The Asperger Paper

While the condition of autism gained worldwide recognition right away, the condition described by Hans Asperger was virtually unheard of anywhere outside of Germany. It wasn't until 1981 when British psychologist Lorna Wing published a paper about Asperger research that the diagnosis was brought to the attention of the English-speaking world. When Wing published her paper, she suggested that the conditions described by Kanner and Asperger were different enough from each other to warrant being called by different names. Wing suggested calling the condition that Asperger had described Asperger syndrome, as opposed to autistic disorder, the term that was used to describe the condition that Kanner had discovered.

Finally, in 1994, a decade after Wing published her paper and fifty years after Hans Asperger discovered the condition, the psychiatric community of the United States listed Asperger as a separate diagnosis for the first time in the *Diagnostic and Statistical Manual of Mental Disorders.*

Still, it took several more years before most professionals were sufficiently familiar with the symptoms associated with the disorder to start identifying it in patients.

Three General Periods

Since its discovery in 1943 by Kanner, doctors have been trying to figure out what causes autism. The history of the theories they have developed about this very complex condition can be divided into three general periods.

Psychoanalysis: The Age of Refrigerator Mothers

At first, experts thought that autism was a psychological condition, meaning they thought it was caused by the circumstances of a person's life. From the late 1940s to the early 1970s, psychiatrists placed the cause for autism right in the laps of mothers. The theory was that in response to feeling unloved and unwanted by their rejecting mothers, children would withdraw into the world of autism. There was even a term coined for these supposedly cold, unloving mothers: "refrigerator mothers."

Biological Explanations

Later, during the 1980s, scientists started to realize that autism had nothing to do with how a child was treated by his or her mother. Eventually, the refrigerator mother theory was completely discredited. The new theory was that autism had nothing to do with psychology of any kind but was instead genetic in origin.

No single cause for autism was found during this period, and to date, none has been discovered. However, evidence began to mount that autism ran in families and that its root causes were biological in nature.

Genetics and Cognitive Science

During the 1990s, most scientists accepted the theory that autism was caused by biological factors, and they began to devote more of their efforts to exploring how genetics could cause autism. At the same time that scientists were looking into the genetic causes of autism, they also started to study the symptoms of autism, specifically the thinking problems common in children with autistic spectrum disorders.

In her autobiographical account of what it is like to have autism, *Thinking in Pictures: And Other Reports from My Life with Autism*, Temple Grandin writes that she still has problems responding quickly to unexpected social situations. She says that when it comes to business, she is usually able to handle most situations, but every now and then she panics when things go wrong. "I have no problems if I mentally rehearse every scenario, but I still panic if I'm not prepared for a new situation, especially when I travel to a foreign country where I am unable to communicate. Since I can't rely on my library of social cues, I feel very helpless when I can't speak the language. Often I withdraw," she writes.

In her autobiography, *Pretending to Be Normal*, Liane Willey, who wasn't diagnosed with Asperger until she was an adult, writes that although she has come a long way in being able to cope with AS, there are many things that still give her difficulty. "I'm really not quite clear with words, what the intent is. I can't tell if they're being straightforward with me. If someone asks me, 'How are you doing today?' I'm going to tell them. And I've been told over and over again, 'They don't really care.'"

Cognitive Theories

The current theories about autism and Asperger syndrome are influenced by a branch of psychology known as cognitive science. Cognitive scientists study the processes that govern human thought and learning.

Since the late 1980s, cognitive science has yielded many insights into the distinctive problems that people with autistic spectrum disorders have with thinking. While these theories do not tell us anything about what causes autism, they do help describe how people on the autistic spectrum think. Specifically, cognitive scientists believe that people with Asperger syndrome have problems with three basic functions of the human brain: executive function, central coherence, and theory of mind.

Executive Function

Whenever we perform a complicated task, we have to pull together a lot of different skills and activities and make them work together. For example, a mother driving a car has to do many things at once—she has to adjust the steering wheel to stay in the lane, pay attention to the signs, plan ahead for turns, watch out for the other cars, and remember where she's going. Most drivers manage to do all this while listening to the radio and trying to quiet down the children in the backseat, and maybe even talking on a cell phone. Cognitive scientists call the mental ability to coordinate several different activities such as these executive function.

Executive function allows us to do more than one thing at a time, and it also helps us make decisions about what to think about. For example, if the mother who is driving the car sees danger ahead—another car veering out of control, for example—chances are she will stop yelling at the kids in the backseat and ignore whatever is being said by the radio announcer. She'll focus all of her attention on avoiding danger. Her executive function ability is what helps her decide, quickly, where she should direct her attention.

Most of us can think of times when we can't manage to focus our attention on the right things; these would be times when our executive function is failing us. For example, our executive function fails us if we daydream when we should be studying or forget about the cake in the oven when the phone rings and we go to answer it. In everyday language, people who hardly ever make these kinds of mistakes are called well organized, and those who are always making mistakes of this nature are called disorganized.

People with Asperger syndrome often have problems with their executive function. The problems show up in many different ways. For example, an AS child who has been sent to her room to get dressed for school might get so caught up in studying a book about geography that was lying on the floor in the hall that she will completely forget about getting dressed. She will be unaware of the fact that if she doesn't get dressed right away, she will not get to school on time. Or, sitting in class, the AS child might be so interested in looking at the crack in the ceiling that is shaped like the state of Florida that he will not even hear what the teacher is saying, even though what he is saying has to do with the scheduling of an exam that will count for half of the final grade.

Other problems with executive function include trouble doing more than one thing at once, becoming easily distracted, and having trouble shifting attention from one task to another.

Central Coherence

Central coherence is the term that cognitive scientists use to describe the ability to look for patterns in things. Central coherence is what enables people to see a field of flowers instead of just an unrelated assortment of colors and shades. Central coherence is what allows people to distinguish the "forest from the trees," so to speak. If people had no central coherence ability at all, they would not be able to make sense of anything. If people had some central coherence but not very much, they might be able to identify objects and understand words but would be totally incapable of understanding situations.

For example, say a person is shown a picture of a little boy who is crying. A woman is patting the boy's shoulder and there is a toy top broken on the floor in front of the boy. What is this a picture of? Most people would say that the child is crying because he has broken his toy and that his mother is trying to comfort him. They'd say this because it's a familiar situation with a familiar cast of characters. They would also come to this conclusion based on their interpretation of the evidence before them: the crying boy, the woman with her hand on his shoulder, the broken toy.

If people's ability for central coherence is weak, they might misinterpret the picture. They might not even notice the broken top. Maybe they would think that the woman was pushing the boy for some unknown reason. Or they might focus on other things having to do with the picture, such as the broken top, the checkered pattern on the woman's dress, or how many buttons the boy has on his shirt. These details might strike people as being more important than the overall picture.

Children with autism and Asperger syndrome often have a problem with central coherence. Of course they are capable of recognizing some patterns in things—thinking would be impossible without some ability to find patterns. They run into trouble when it comes to grasping the main point of a story or what another person might be feeling or thinking in a particular situation.

So, although most children with Asperger syndrome learn to read quickly and develop large vocabularies, they sometimes have big problems with reading comprehension. Their problem with reading comprehension will show up on tests where they are asked to give the main idea of a story or to pick the best title for it. A child with Asperger syndrome may remember every detail of the story but will still not be able to get the point of it.

The fact that they have so much difficulty with central coherence may explain why so many children with AS have such a need for order and why they are so drawn to the tools that human beings have invented to make sense of the world—tools like maps, alphabets, encyclopedias, and lists. When facts are ordered in a strict way, the patterns are much easier to see.

Theory of Mind

People all experience their own thoughts and feelings. But what about other people's thoughts and feelings? They cannot actually experience other people's thoughts and feelings, can they? Then how do they know that other people think and feel things, too?

Cognitive scientists have concluded that at a certain point in early childhood, most children realize that other people have thoughts and feelings of their own. They call this realization theory of mind. Once children realize that other people have thoughts, they start to spend a lot of time trying to guess what those thoughts might be. For example, a four-year-old will see her mother frowning and think, "Is Mommy mad at me? What did I do to make her mad?" Or, climbing the monkey bars, she will call out to her mother to look at her because she wants her mother to be paying attention to her.

When children develop theory of mind, it becomes very important to them to share their experiences with other people. Having this ability makes people more sociable. Not having theory of mind would tend to make a person solitary—it might make him feel that he is the only person in the world.

Theory of mind isn't just a belief that people have about other people. It's a skill that children start developing at a very early age. The sooner they realize that other people have thoughts and feelings of their own, the more time they will have to develop the skill of figuring out what other people are thinking and the more skillful they will be at developing relationships.

Children with AS are capable of understanding that other people have minds of their own, but when it comes to trying to figure out what other people might actually be thinking, they tend to make many mistakes. This inability to figure out what people are thinking is why they often say things that may seem inappropriate in social situations, things that might embarrass or hurt other people, things that might reflect unfavorably on themselves. This may also be why people with AS might go on and on talking about something without even realizing that the person they are talking to isn't the slightest bit interested in what they are saying. People with AS are just not very good at reading the clues that tell most people what somebody else is thinking or feeling. It is almost as if they lack a sense that most people have. Some cognitive scientists have labeled this condition mindblindness.

The Needs of People with Asperger

In an interview in the *New Yorker* magazine in 1993, Dr. Temple Grandin said that the experience of having autism was like being "an anthropologist on Mars."[1]

Dr. Grandin, who is an assistant professor of animal sciences and an award-winning engineer, has spent her life constructing an elaborate system of cues and symbols that allows her to function in a society that is as alien to her as ours might be to someone from Mars. Dr. Grandin has written extensively about what it feels like to have autism, and she travels around the world giving lectures about it.

A Lot of Hard Work

People with AS say that learning social skills is something they have to be constantly working on. "People know when to talk, when not to talk, and for how long," says Jerry Newport, who wasn't diagnosed with AS until he was an adult. "They know how to read the nods and smiles, to know when someone's really listening to you or just enduring you."[2]

Many people have published articles on Asperger syndrome. They have also posted their thoughts on the Internet. Children as young as ten years old have published books about their experiences. Here is a sample of what they have to say about what it feels like to have Asperger syndrome and high functioning autism.

➪ *My hearing is like having a hearing aid with the volume control stuck on "super loud." It is like an open microphone that picks up everything.* —Temple Grandin[3]

➪ *The biggest problem for me is that I am misunderstood by teachers and other people. They think I am purposely being rude, or being lazy (as with my handwriting). They think that I don't care about things. I do care. I just don't understand. I am not trying to make people's lives hard. In addition, I misinterpret things that people say and get my feelings hurt. People don't see a wheelchair or any other visual sign of disability so they assume nothing is wrong with me.* —Alexander Plank[4]

➪ *It seems to me that society as a whole is actually more rigid than AS people. Having an AS kid in the family can actually be very good for the whole family, as it surely must make the relatives revise their whole way of looking at the world.* —Nicholas Barrow[5]

➪ *AS is an irremovable part of a person. Imagine placing a layer of peanut butter on top of a piece of bread, and then a layer of jelly on top of that, and then another layer of peanut butter. The layer of jelly is analogous to a person's Asperger syndrome. An attempt to remove the layer of jelly smoothly would prove to be impossible.* —Eric Chen[6]

Many people with Asperger report that with time and training and a lot of practice, they have been able to learn how to navigate themselves around the social world. In *A Survival Guide for People with Asperger*, Mark Segar wrote that he now has social interaction "down to a science." He continued, "However, there is one thing I must make an effort never to forget and that is what it's like to suffer from Asperger syndrome."[7]

The Importance of Education

While there might someday be a pill that can help children with Asperger syndrome be less obsessive and pay more attention in class, the only way they will learn what they need to know to get along in the world is through education. Children with Asperger have to learn in a formal way—through books and pictures, through worksheets and structured play—things that other kids learn just by hanging out with each other in the cafeteria or on the playground.

For children with Asperger syndrome, education is a kind of medicine—it is the best-known treatment for the disorder, and it is crucial that the children be given the kind of education that can help them learn how to cope with the symptoms of AS.

Individuals with Disabilities Education Act (IDEA)

Meeting the needs of children with AS is the responsibility of the local board of education, which, according to a law called the Individuals with Disabilities Education Act (IDEA), must give all children with disabilities a free and appropriate education. This means that the board must do whatever is necessary to educate children, no matter how expensive or time-consuming it might turn out to be.

But just because this is the law doesn't mean that educating people with Asperger always works out so smoothly. Meeting the needs of children with Asperger has proven to be a particularly difficult problem since most school districts have been designed to deal with children who have educational needs that are very different from those of children with AS.

In order to get services for their children, parents often end up having to take legal action against their school districts. As a result of the conflict between parents and school boards, school districts across the country are spending hundreds of thousands of dollars a year on legal battles, fighting parents who are demanding services for their children. This is money that otherwise could be spent educating children.[8]

A Hidden Disability

In class, the child with Asperger syndrome will often be the bright kid with a "behavior problem." She might rock in her chair, hum incessantly to herself, or drum her fingers on the table. It often seems as though she isn't paying any attention to what the teacher is saying, yet she often gets very high grades, and when it comes to subjects like geography and math, she is often way ahead of her classmates.

Seeing a child who looks a little strange but isn't failing, a teacher is not likely to think she has any special problems that would require special attention. As a result, the AS child's real educational needs—her need to learn the "social curriculum"—are often ignored. It is easy for a teacher to see why a student who is failing math needs extra help, but it is not so easy for him to see why a child who doesn't know how to have a conversation, a child who can't pack up his backpack or keep track of his papers, or a child who spends all of his recesses alone might need extra help as well. But when it comes to children with Asperger, learning how to fit in socially is just as important as academics, if not more so.

Educating the School System

Since Asperger is so new in terms of its being a separate, established psychiatric diagnosis in the United States, many school systems are not even aware of the fact that it exists at all. If they are aware of it, they often do not understand it.

Complicating the problem even further is the fact that the educational institutions that are designed to train teachers and therapists to work with children with special needs are not training them to work with children with AS. "We desperately need a systematic way to teach educators about this disability," says Dr. Brenda Smith Myles, who teaches the only graduate-level AS training program in the country. "These children are so complicated and they have so many contradictions that unless teachers really know what they are doing, they could completely miss what the real problem is and therefore miss the opportunity of giving the child the help he or she needs."[9]

As a result of the prevailing ignorance that exists about Asperger, it often falls on parents to educate their schools about it. They have to explain why a child who is getting straight As in every subject is getting straight Fs on the playground. They have to explain to the school system that there are subjects that children with AS need to learn, subjects that are not included in the regular curriculum. They have to explain that it is just as important for their children to learn the social curriculum as it is for them to learn math or geography.

Learning the Social Curriculum

Despite the fact that he has a huge vocabulary and can talk at great length about his areas of special interest, a child with AS often needs help with the social aspects of language. He often needs training in the give-and-take of carrying on a conversation. He needs to learn how to play games, how to deal with teasing, and how to have friends. Taken together, the learning of these skills is what is known as the social curriculum. It is also known as the hidden curriculum, since it does not include subjects on which children are usually graded or judged.

"What we take for granted, the student with Asperger has to be taught—and taught and taught over and over again in different ways so that it will make an impression on him strong enough for him to remember it and to know how to apply it to real life situations," says Ronee Groff, president of the Learning Disabilities Association. "They need a whole curriculum of that. Learning the hidden curriculum is more important for the child with Asperger than it is for him or her to learn reading, writing, or math. The hidden curriculum is vital in order for him to learn how to apply what he learns, whatever he learns, in a useful way."[10]

A Team Effort

Teaching the social curriculum to the child with AS is not just the work of one teacher—it is the work of a team of experts. This team includes a behavioral specialist who knows how to look at and analyze behavior, a developmental specialist who understands normal development and can set goals for the child that are appropriate for his age, and a language specialist, since children with Asperger have such severe language problems.

Depending on the child, there might be other problems, such as anxiety or depression, that need to be addressed by an expert as well. It is essential that every one of the child's needs be addressed. To neglect one area of need would amount to neglecting them all. "If a child is taught just a little bit of this and a little bit of that, it never comes together," says Dr. Vicki Sudhalter, a psychologist who specializes in the language problems of children with Asperger.[11] All this important learning that the child with AS has to do is supposed to take place in school. Dr. Raun Melmed says that children "might as well just stay home if they can't learn from social curriculum in an environment that can accept them."[12]

Better Understanding of the Difference Between Asperger and Autism

Confusion about the relationship between Asperger syndrome and autism often makes it difficult for educators to know how to respond to the needs of children who have these disorders. Is Asperger the same as autism, or is it an altogether different disability? Are children with Asperger syndrome handicapped or aren't they? If they are, how handicapped are they? All this can be even more confusing because there is so much variation in the amount of help the children need, with some children needing a lot of help and others very little.

Sometimes it seems that every bit of help has to be fought for. The parents of children with Asperger syndrome often use words like "struggle," "battle," and "fight" when they are talking about their dealings with their local school boards. One mother coined the term "guerilla mom" to describe what it is like being the mother of a child with a disability and having to fight constantly for services for your child.

Sadly, many parents say that trying to convince educators of their children's need for help is the most difficult aspect of having a child with Asperger. As one mother puts it, "Eventually the shock of the diagnosis wears off and you just work with your child. Every step that he makes, the slightest sign of progress, are all cause for rejoicing. What

71

I can't deal with, what I can never get used to, is this constant wrangling over services."[13]

Not Enough Services

In some cases, the school administrators charged with the responsibility of giving services to children with special needs do not consider AS to be a serious condition. When they hear that a child has problems with social skills, they might think that such problems do not even fall within the scope of their responsibilities. They may refuse to give the child any help, not give him or her enough, or give him or her the wrong kind of help.

If they think that a child's difficulties are caused by autism, they will probably realize the child needs help, but that, too, could lead to a whole different set of confusions and another set of battles between the parents and the school board.

Inappropriate Placements

Educational evaluators who think of Asperger syndrome in terms of autism often fail to appreciate the great range of differences that exist among children who are considered to be on the "autistic spectrum." In their minds, it makes sense to lump all children together. The mother of one child with AS tells how her school district recommended that her child be placed in a classroom for children with moderate to severe autism and mental retardation. The district based its recommendation on the fact that the AS child had the same classification as all the other children in the class—autistic. It failed to consider the fact that the child's symptoms were far less severe than those of the other children in the class.

The consequences of such a placement would have been tragic for this child. Instead of learning how to behave in ways that were more socially appropriate, he would have learned how to behave in ways that were inappropriate. Instead of learning how to control himself and respect the rights of others, he would have learned how to bang his head against the wall and have temper tantrums. And he would not have been given access to learning that was anywhere near his potential.

Since children with Asperger syndrome often get very upset for no apparent reason, they are sometimes mistakenly placed in special education classes designed for children who are "emotionally disturbed." Children with Asperger syndrome might act in ways that bear some resemblance to the behavior of children who are emotionally disturbed, but the cause of their problems have altogether different roots and they are altogether different kinds of children.

Children with AS tend to be very naive and gentle; emotionally disturbed children tend to be very aggressive, sometimes even violent. Putting these children together is a recipe for disaster. Dr. Fred Volkmar of Yale University says that placing a child with AS in a classroom with children who are emotionally disturbed is the worst possible fate for the child. He says it amounts to surrounding the "perfect victim" with the "perfect victimizers."[14]

Deciding on a Placement

The ideal classroom environment for a child with AS is one that is small enough for the teacher to be able to respond directly to the child's needs and one in which there is a mix of children with special needs and mainstream students, so that the child with AS is able to have neurotypical children as models for appropriate behavior. However, the fact is that the ideal environment rarely, if ever, exists for the child with AS. When it comes to choosing a school for their children, parents are often surprised to discover that there are few, if any, choices available to them.

Parents are often faced with the choice of either putting their child in a special education school—a school that is specifically designed to meet the needs of handicapped children—or of placing their child in a mainstream classroom, in which the children are not disabled. Both of these choices have their drawbacks.

Mainstream Classrooms

Mainstream classrooms can have many distractions, they tend to be very large (some can have more than thirty children), and the teachers are neither trained nor equipped to handle the needs of a child with Asperger. Also, since the child with AS tends to be the only child with a disability in the classroom, his strange behaviors can be very conspicuous to his fellow classmates; this results in the child being shunned by his classmates or worse.

Special Education Schools

Special education schools and classrooms tend to be much less challenging for children. According to some parents, many special education schools and class-rooms are nothing more than warehouses for children. Mary Clancy, the mother of an eleven-year-old with autism, recalls that when her son was diagnosed with autism, she and her husband went searching for a school for him. "The first thing we noticed about these schools was that they were uniformly dank and dark," Clancy says. "They all echoed with the sounds of shrieking children. There was no teaching going on. Walking out of each of these places, my husband and I would look at each other in horror and say 'not our kid.' How could you put anyone you loved in a place like that?" Clancy reports that since there was no viable alternative, she had to spend the next seven years educating her son at home.[15]

A Balancing Act

Making the right decision regarding a placement often comes down to choosing the lesser of two evils. "It's so difficult to find the right school for my son," says Barbara Oxenfeldt. "It's almost an impossibility, so you have to compromise." Oxenfeldt says that the problem she and her husband have had is that they don't want to fall into the trap of putting their son in a classroom with kids who have problems just like his. "Then he wouldn't learn from the other kids, and he wouldn't get the social modeling he needs," she explains. "On the other hand, we don't want to throw him into a situation where there will be too many demands placed on him. So where do we go? It's a constant balancing act."[16]

Tutoring at Home

Since the special education curriculum is often not sufficiently challenging for children with AS, parents often find themselves in the position of having to offer their children extra tutoring at home to supplement what they are supposed to be learning at school. Oxenfeldt says that special education schools rarely give enough homework and rarely offer enough extracurricular activities, so she is constantly having to generate homework for her child and sign him up for activities so that he will be able to use his time productively.

Coping with
Asperger at School

In her book *The Stolen Child: Aspects of Autism and Asperger Syndrome*, Ann Hewetson tells the story of a boy with AS who felt so overwhelmed by the environment of school that he would withdraw into himself and go into "shutdown"—feeling nothing, seeing nothing, hearing nothing. Hewetson writes that the boy said he had no control over his reaction, which he would compare to a television station going off the air. He said it felt as if "somebody had just turned off the switch."[1]

The mere act of sitting in a classroom and dealing with the many distractions that exist within the school environment can be very difficult for children with AS. The steam coming up through the radiator, the sound of kids joking with each other outside in the hall, the artwork on the walls—these are just a few of the things that can distract the AS child from focusing on what he or she is supposed to be doing.

Understanding Social Priorities

Going to school presents many challenges to the student with AS. Waiting at the bus stop, sitting down at their desks and getting out the materials that are required for the lesson, taking notes, moving from class to class, taking down

A Few Lessons for School

Children with Asperger should learn how to do the following.

- ➪ Use nonverbal communication to express emotion

- ➪ Identify nonverbal communication in others

- ➪ Follow the basic social dos and don'ts

- ➪ Make and keep friends

- ➪ Identify sarcasm and distinguish good-natured teasing from bullying

- ➪ Respond to social questions

homework assignments—these are tasks that require students with AS to make extensive use of abilities that they have the most trouble utilizing.

Students have to realize that if they are late for class, they might miss something and be penalized for it. They have to realize that they are supposed to say hello to people who say hello to them and come up with some kind of small talk that would serve as a socially appropriate response. Students have to understand that other people might not be interested in the same things they're interested in and might not like the same things they like. Therefore, they have to understand that they can't insist on having everything their own way all the time. They can't insist that the teacher always talk about what they are interested in hearing about at the moment. They also can't insist on lecturing other people about their special interests.

Schoolwork

While children with AS often excel academically, learning tends to become more of a problem in the upper grades, where more critical thinking skills are required. Students with Asperger will have problems interpreting literature and understanding subjects like sociology and psychology, which often call on students to analyze emotions or to describe people's characters.

"They don't even understand how they themselves feel in a particular context, so how can they infer what a character portrayed in a piece of literature might be feeling?" points out Vivian Polo, a reading specialist with an expertise in working with children with Asperger.

Polo says that an important first step to improving a child's reading comprehension is for him to be excited about reading. For children with AS, reading about their areas of special interest is a good place to start. "You want the child to love to read," says Polo. "They want to know everything they can about whatever their passion is. What they want to learn about they will want to read about. That should be exploited for every penny it's worth." By reading things that are of interest to him, the child's overall level of reading comprehension can be improved. Once his comprehension level is up, he can start reading literature, bit by bit.

In order to get children with AS to the point where they will be ready to interpret literature, they have to continually increase their awareness of the world around them. They have to constantly see the world of emotions. They have to label their own emotions and the emotions of other people so that they will eventually be able to relate what they are reading about to what is happening in the context of their lives. "It's not as if there is a reading section in their minds," says Polo.

Since Asperger is a disorder that makes people see the world in such a different way, teachers have to understand that a child with AS is not going to learn in the same way that most people learn. There is no one magic key. Each child has his own key. It is the teacher's job to try new keys and make up keys that never existed before. "As a teacher, you better learn Martian if you're going to succeed in teaching the child with AS," says Polo.[2]

A reading tutor who has been trained to address the kinds of problems that are unique to children with AS can devise specific strategies to help them compensate for their particular areas of deficit. The following are some techniques for learning reading.

⇨ Relate what is being read to something that has happened in the child's life.

⇨ Copy the reading material and highlight all the emotion words and all the action words. Then reread the material. Now all those words will pop out at the student and she will have a better understanding of their meaning.

↩ Depending on the reading level, stop throughout the text and ask questions about what he is reading: "Why is he happy?" "Why did she do that?" "How was he feeling?" There has to be a constant give-and-take for the information.

↩ Do not assume the child is understanding something just because the other children understand it.

↩ The child should learn how to analyze people's individual characteristics by learning about stereotypes.

Dealing with Teasing

The "odd" child with the unusual behaviors makes an ideal target for bullying and teasing. Some children with AS won't even realize they are being teased, whereas for others it will be the source of their greatest grief.

Since children respond so differently to teasing, there is no single approach that will work. But there are some general rules that can be followed. First, the child should never respond directly to the tease—he should just walk away from it or he should be helped to find a way of responding to it that will suit his own personality and sense of dignity. If it looks like the teasing is getting out of hand, he should be taught that he needs to bring the matter to the attention of someone in charge.

The following are some general guidelines for handling teasing.

⇨ Try to prevent the teasing from happening in the first place by removing the causes for teasing as much as possible. The child with AS should always be well groomed and dressed in the current style and should be given ongoing training in social skills.

⇨ The AS child should be in an environment that will be friendly toward him or her. The AS child should be in a classroom of children who are well behaved and who are interested in learning. If the children are not nice, then they have to be taught to be nice. It is also important that the child's classmates be tolerant of other people's differences.

⇨ The AS child should learn what it means to be teased. Often the child with AS will not understand when she is being teased. She might take playful teasing seriously or she might totally miss the fact that other children are making fun of her. She needs to learn the difference between playful teasing and hostile teasing.

What Can Be Done?

How much help a child with AS needs will depend on what his or her particular problems are. At one end of the spectrum is the child who has relatively mild Asperger syndrome. If his problems are not so severe that they will prevent him from making it through the school day on his own, then he might not require many supports—social skills training or therapy to help him with his speech might be sufficient.

Intensive Support

There are many children with AS, however, who require a very intensive level of support. Falling into this category are children who have problems with the following.

- ⮎ Paying attention

- ⮎ Auditory processing

- ⮎ Social skills

- ⮎ Controlling their impulses

- ⮎ Organization skills

- ⮎ Working independently

- ⮎ Expressing themselves

Children like this might require the services of a full-time aide, someone who can help them do whatever is necessary to get through the day. These students might also require additional therapies, such as speech therapy, occupational therapy, and counseling.

Year-Round Services

Some children with Asperger syndrome have such an enormous amount of catching up to do in terms of their social and communication skills that they require help all year. "Many children with Asperger cannot afford to take the summer off," says Dr. Bridget Taylor, a prominent expert on autism. "They have to learn social skills every day of the week, 365 days of the year, weekends and vacations included. The summer months often need to be devoted to maintaining and building on their social skills."[3]

Dr. Jed Baker points out, "There is a big difference between learning a concept and learning how to apply the skill spontaneously. Some children can learn the skill during a fifteen-minute session on a Monday morning. But the prompting of that skill, the coaching of it, and teaching the child how to anticipate when, where, and how to use it—that needs to happen every day, 365 days of the year, for some children."[4]

Legally, the local board of education is required to address the social needs of children as much as it is required to address problems with reading or math. "If a child doesn't greet people, if he can't have a conversation, if he doesn't have any friends, or if he doesn't know how to stay on topic, then that child cannot afford to take any time off. It's not a negotiable issue," says Dr. Brenda Smith Myles.[5]

Consultants

It is quite possible that most of the child's teachers, including the specialists who have been assigned to work with him or her, will not be familiar with Asperger syndrome. For this reason, it is essential that someone who has had a lot of experience working with children with AS be hired to make sure that all the people who are working with the child are doing what they need to be doing to help him or her.

The consultant identifies the child's needs and devises strategies for helping the child achieve his or her goals. He acts as the team leader, meeting on a regular basis with the people who are working with the child and making sure that everyone is on the right track. The consultant is constantly setting new goals and raising the bar to make sure that the child is always being challenged to achieve his or her potential.

Aides

If a child needs a full-time aide, the aide should have intensive training, and this training needs to be given on an ongoing basis. "An aide who hasn't been well trained or one who is not a good match for the child can be worse for the child than having no aide at all," says Dr. Bridget Taylor. For example, an aide who tries to do too much for the child or "overprompts" him could make him so dependent on support that he will end up relying on the aide to do everything for him, even things that he might otherwise be able to do for himself. This kind of approach would totally defeat the purpose of the aide, points out Dr. Taylor. "The overall goal of the aide is to promote independent functioning so that the child is responding to the natural cues—the teachers or classmates—instead of just to her prompts," she says.[6]

Working on Strengths as Well as Weaknesses

Children with Asperger often have many strengths and sometimes great gifts. Educators try to take a child's strengths and build them to use as a foundation to address the child's weaknesses. "There are many examples of children with AS or high functioning autism who grew up to be successful adults," says Geraldine Dawson, coauthor of *A Parent's Guide to Asperger Syndrome and High-Functioning Autism.* "The key was their being able to use their strengths . . . This can help them blossom rather than flounder."[7]

One mistake that special educators often make is that they think so much in terms of the child's diagnosis that they lose sight of her strengths. Barbara Oxenfeldt says that one of the things she likes best about her son's school is that they never use the word "Asperger." "I'm thrilled about that, because as far as I'm concerned, the differences between the children with AS far outnumber the similarities. The AS label doesn't help when dealing with specific problems," she says.[8]

"Often, we put too much emphasis on the disabled area. You have to focus on the skills you are good at and figure out how to use them to work around your disability," says Temple Grandin, who says she owes her success to teachers who encouraged her to develop her area of talent.[9]

How Other Children Help

When a child with Asperger is included in a mainstream class, teachers try to formally enlist the help of the other children in the class. The child's classmates can be his most valuable helpers. When choosing children to act as the AS child's helpers, teachers look for children who are kind and empathetic. They also select children who are well respected by their classmates. Having a popular kid hang out with a kid with AS can have a ripple effect. The other kids will want to copy what the popular kid is doing. The idea is that if you have one or two popular kids hanging around the child, before long you will have five kids hanging around him, all wanting to pitch in and help.

Children with AS should learn the following conversation skills.

- Maintain an appropriate distance (not too close, not too far).

- Maintain appropriate body language (for example, no excessive slouching or grimacing).

- Maintain appropriate eye contact when talking with a peer.

- Refrain from inappropriate touching.

- Acknowledge the other person's statements.

- Refrain from interrupting or cutting off.

- Listen to what the other person says.

- Stay on topic (no abrupt shifts in topic or jumping around).

- Bring up a new topic gracefully.

- Leave old topics behind when the topic of conversation has changed.

- Stay attuned to what the other person finds interesting.

- Allow others to take turns talking.

- Refrain from talking over the other person.

- End the conversation gracefully.

- Maintain an appropriate volume.[10]

There are a number of different things that other children can do to help the child with AS.

- ⇌ Greet the child when he enters the classroom.

- ⇌ Sit next to the child in class and help her participate in group activities.

- ⇌ Engage him in play or conversation during recess.

- ⇌ Eat lunch with her.

- ⇌ Walk him home.

"Rather than pick on the child with AS or tease him when he does annoying things, the nondisabled child can give him constructive criticism on how he can improve his social skills," says Lori Shery. "For another kid to say to a child with AS, 'I don't like when you do that. It makes me feel creeped out and I would rather you stood further back when you talked to me,' would be of true value to the AS child and a welcome alternative to the teasing that takes place."[11]

How the Teacher Helps

In his original paper about Asperger syndrome in 1944, Hans Asperger said that the children he studied were very sensitive to the personality of the teacher—"surprisingly so," he said. He stressed the importance of the teacher's role in reaching the children. "They can be taught, but only by those who give them true understanding and affection, people who show kindness toward them and, yes, humor . . . The teacher's underlying emotional attitude influences,

Aides help the AS child realize his or her potential, whatever that may be. The aide constantly helps the child develop new skills, with the ultimate goal being independence. How well the aide does his or her job can mean whether the child succeeds or fails in school.

The following are some of the duties of the aide.

⮞ Providing emotional support to the child

⮞ Helping the child with organization

⮞ Giving the child "incidental" instruction on social skills throughout the course of the day

⮞ Monitoring the child's behavior and giving him or her consistent feedback on what he or she is doing well and what needs to be worked on

⮞ Making the child aware of what is happening around him or her in order to learn from the surrounding environment

⮞ Teaching the child how to pick up on nonverbal cues

⮞ Helping the child learn how to play with other children on the playground

involuntarily and unconsciously, the mood and behavior of the child."[12]

The teacher's behavior toward the child with AS also influences how he is perceived by his fellow students. It is therefore imperative that the teacher support him in every way she can.

Here are some tips on how the teacher should treat the child with AS.

- Being sincere and respectful of the student

- Recognizing the child's strengths and gifts and working with them

- Praising worthy accomplishments in a sincere manner

- Respecting individual differences

- Protecting the student from bullying by educating his peers

- Communicating frequently with the other teachers and parents about what areas the child is making progress in and what areas he still needs to work on

- Watching out for the pitfall of being so focused on the child's deficit that the teacher fails to address his areas of strength, which need to be supported as well[13]

Working with Parents

Lori Shery says that the first thing she tells parents when they call her for help is that there is hope and that it's going to get better: "I tell them that there are just some obstacles in the way and that they have to think differently about getting around things. I tell them their child will most likely be fine. They just need to know what they need to get there."[1]

Hearing that there is hope for their children is a great source of comfort for parents, and it continues to be one of their greatest sources of comfort as the years progress and they watch their children growing and improving, little by little. Parents cling to the hope that one day their children will grow up and have meaningful careers, will be able to get married and have families, and will have a chance of living independent, productive, and happy lives. This is what spurs them on to do everything within their power to see to it that their children are at least given a fighting chance of one day having these hopes realized.

If hope is the greatest source of comfort for parents, then doing whatever they can to get their children the help they need is the greatest form of therapy. "Most parents are devastated [by the diagnosis] and the impact on the family is great," write the authors of *A Parent's Guide to Asperger Syndrome and High-Functioning Autism.* "But many parents rally and are able to start on this journey to find their child." However, the authors caution, parents have to realize that the journey is not going to be a short one. "They need to know this process is a distance race, not a sprint."[2]

An Awesome Task

The parents of children with Asperger syndrome face an awesome task. To begin with, they must learn everything they can about a disability for which there is a lot of confusing and conflicting information. Then, in the face of a great deal of contradictory advice, they have to decide what course of treatment would be best for their child. And then there is the long, hard struggle to secure services. All of this entails an incredible amount of work.

No one really knows what the future holds for a child with AS. All that is known is that the more work that is put into the child when he is still young, the better his chances are for the future. The effort that parents make to help their children can mean all the difference in how their children's lives ultimately turn out. Parents know this, and they know that the harder they work, the better the chances are that their children will one day grow up to live free and independent lives.

"I don't think anyone but the parent of a child with a disability can realize how great a catastrophe such an occurrence can be in the life of a family," says the mother of a seven-year-old with AS. "In the case of Asperger, I believe it is even more difficult to imagine what is involved, since autism, if caught early enough and dealt with rigorously enough, is a disability that can be remediated with varying degrees of success. With an autistic child, you never know how far you can go, until you try."[3]

Parents: The Only Experts

Since Asperger is a disorder that comes in so many different forms, professionals couldn't possibly have enough time to familiarize themselves with all the needs of each individual child. Only the parents can do that. Only parents know all their child's strengths and weaknesses. Only they know what their child is capable of doing. Only they know what kinds of approaches will ultimately work with their child and what will be best for him or her.

"You will become an expert in your child's abilities and disabilities, making decisions about which treatments to try, and educating teachers, service providers and others about your child," write the authors of *A Parent's Guide to Asperger Syndrome and High-Functioning Autism.*[4]

Still, despite the crucial role that they have to play in their children's treatment, parents are often not asked to contribute to decisions regarding their children's treatment and care. Often they have to fight to be heard by educators who think they have all the answers.

One of the most important things that an educator has to learn is that the parent can be one of his or her most important resources. Most experts agree that Asperger syndrome is a condition that requires a strong collaboration between parents and professionals.[5]

A Life-Changing Experience

Figuring out what is best for the child and then trying to convince the board of education to provide the help that he or she needs can be a very expensive and time-consuming process.

"Having an autistic child will change everything about your life—from whether you get enough sleep at night to how likely you are to get divorced," writes Mitzi Waltz, author of the book *Autistic Spectrum Disorders*. "It's hugely stressful, and that's not helped by the lack of help from medical professionals, schools and social services agencies. Indeed, the situation for many families is horrendous."[6]

Many parents end up having to give up successful careers, sell their homes, or go into bankruptcy in order to take care of their children. The costs in emotional and physical terms are also enormous. "I go to sleep with it and wake up in the middle of the night thinking about it. I dream about it, and the first thing I do every morning before the children wake up is sit down at the computer and get to work on pulling it all together," says Margaret Benjamin, the mother of an eleven-year-old with Asperger.

Benjamin says that she feels that 90 percent of her time is spent trying to get the board of education to give her son the services he needs. This is very stressful for her and her family. "I find I have much less patience for my son. I have less time for him. What's more, this constant badgering away at the board of education trying to convince them how disabled my son is affects how I perceive him. It makes me so focused on his disability that I begin to see him in terms of his disorder instead of in terms of the wonderful, amazing little boy that he is. That's what I hate most about this constant fighting over services. That's the very worst part of it all—what it does to my relationship with my son," she says.[7]

However, almost every parent will say that despite all the pain and hardship, the joy of having a child with AS far outweighs the sorrows. This is important for the child to understand. Ultimately, there is no greater source of support or comfort for parents than the love they have for their children. Love is the force behind everything they do. It is what keeps their hopes and dreams alive during the darkest and most difficult times.

CEO of Jimmy Inc.

The mother of one child jokes about how taking care of her boy Jimmy, who has Asperger syndrome, is like being the CEO of Jimmy Inc. But when she made a list of all the things she does in her role as Jimmy's mother, she saw that there was a lot more truth to this than she first realized.

- ⮱ In her role as advocate, she has to make sure that Jimmy gets the help he needs.

- ⮱ In her role as teacher, she constantly has to try out new ways of explaining the world of people to him in ways that he will understand.

- ⮱ In her role as therapist, she constantly has to create new strategies for him, to cope with his deficits, and she has to constantly monitor his progress and move on to new goals and objectives.

☞ In her role as protector, she has to stick up for her child when he is misunderstood or treated unfairly by his teachers or his fellow students.

☞ In her role as scholar and researcher, she has to be on the lookout for new ideas and new therapies that might help him, search for new people who might be able to help him, and search for schools that might be able to address his complex needs.

☞ In her role as personnel director, she has to evaluate the people who are working with her son, making sure that they are doing their jobs well, and if they are not, she has to find new people to replace them.

☞ In her role as secretary, she has to keep track of all his appointments, as well as keep records of the money that is owed and money that has been paid. She also has to think up ways to get more money when she doesn't have any more available.

☞ In her role as diplomat, if her child inadvertently hurts someone's feelings or if he gets into trouble of some kind, she has to step in and smooth things over so that her child will not have to suffer too much for his mistakes.

☞ In her role as friend, she has to play with her child when there is no one else for him to play with, and she always has to look for things that will be fun for him to do.

➥ In her role as policewoman, she has to make sure he doesn't do things that could be dangerous to himself or other people, and if he does, she has to make sure he learns not to do it again.

➥ But, above all, in her role as parent, she has to appreciate her child for who he is and love him with all her heart.

Children with Asperger can learn how to cope with their difficulties if they get the kind of help they need. This entails a lot of hard work for parents and educators. It also entails a lot of hard work for the children themselves.

But the fact is that in order for children with AS to have any chance at succeeding in the world, they need to adapt to the ways of the rest of the world. As difficult as this task might be, there are many people who have managed to tackle the job successfully, and many of them agree that it was worth the hard work.

Glossary

attention deficit hyperactivity disorder (ADHD) A condition characterized by disorganization, an inability to concentrate, being easily distracted, impulsiveness, and hyperactivity.

autism A complex neurological disorder that causes problems with verbal and nonverbal communication and social interaction.

behaviorism The viewpoint that behavior is the appropriate subject matter for psychological study.

cognitive science A relatively new area of study that focuses on how people learn, rather than what they learn.

critical thinking The mental process of acquiring information, then evaluating it to reach a logical conclusion or answer.

curriculum The subject matter that teachers and students cover in class.

dyslexia A reading disorder that causes people to transpose letters, have difficulty recognizing letters or numbers, and have poor handwriting.

intelligence quotient (IQ) A test designed to reflect a person's mental capacities.

learning disability A condition that results in a discrepancy between a person's intelligence and academic achievement.

modeling Showing a student how to do a task with the expectation that he or she will copy the model.

neurologist A doctor specializing in medical conditions associated with the nervous system, specifically the brain and spinal cord.

neurotypical A term used to refer to people who are neurologically normal.

nonverbal learning disability (NLD) A learning difference that is categorized by strong verbal abilities and poor social skills.

obsessive-compulsive disorder (OCD) A disorder that causes a person to repeat certain acts in order to relieve anxiety.

refrigerator mother Term previously used to describe mothers of autistic children who were believed to have caused their children's autism by acting coldly.

special education Programs designed to serve children with mental and physical disabilities.

theory of mind The ability to understand that others' thoughts, beliefs, desires, and intentions are different from one's own.

Where to Go for Help

In the United States

Asperger Syndrome Coalition of the
  U.S. (ASC-US)
2020 Pennsylvania Avenue NW
Box 771
Washington, DC 20006
(866) 4-ASPRGR (427-7747)
Web site: http://www.asc-us.org

Autism Society of America
7910 Woodmont Avenue, Suite 300
Bethesda, MD 20814-3067
(301) 657-0881
(800) 3-AUTISM (328-8476)
e-mail: info@autism-society.org
Web site: http://www.autism-society.org

Learning Disabilities Association of
  America (LDA)
4156 Library Road
Pittsburgh, PA 15234-1349
(412) 341-1515
Web site: http://www.ldanatl.org

MAAP Services—The Autism Source
P.O. Box 524
Crown Point, IN 46307
(219) 662-1311
Web site: http://www.maapservices.org

National Information Center for Children and Youth
 with Disabilities (NICHCY)
P.O. Box 1492
Washington, DC 20013-1492
(800) 695-0285
e-mail: nichcy@aed.org
Web site: http://www.nichcy.org

National Institute of Neurological Disorders and
 Stroke (NINDS)
P.O. Box 5801
Bethesda, MD 20824
(800) 352-9424
Web site: http://www.ninds.nih.gov

In Canada

Autism Society Ontario
179 A King Street, Suite 004
Toronto, ON M6K 3C5
(416) 246-9592
e-mail: mail@autismsociety.on.ca
Web site: http://www.autismsociety.on.ca

Canadian Institutes of Health Research
410 Laurier Avenue W., 9th Floor
Address Locator 4209A
Ottawa, ON K1A 0W9
(888) 603-4178
e-mail: info@cihr-irsc.gc.ca
Web site: http://www.cihr-irsc.gc.ca

Health Canada
A.L. 0900C2
Ottawa, ON K1A 0K9
(613) 957-2991
e-mail: info@hc-sc.gc.ca
Web site: http://www.hc-sc.gc.ca

Web Sites

Due to the changing nature of Internet links, the Rosen Publishing Group, Inc., has developed an online list of Web sites related to the subject of this book. This site is updated regularly. Please use this link to access the list:

http://www.rosenlinks.com/cop/assy

For Further Reading

Bleach, Fiona. *Everybody Is Different: A Book for Young People Who Have Brothers or Sisters with Autism.* Shawnee Mission, KS: Autism Asperger Publishing Company, 2002.

Ives, Martine. *What Is Asperger Syndrome, and How Will It Affect Me?* Shawnee Mission, KS: Austism Asperger Publishing Company, 2002.

Ledgin, Norm, and Temple Grandin. *Asperger's and Self-Esteem: Insight and Hope Through Famous Role Models.* Arlington, TX: Future Horizons, 2002.

Myles, Brenda Smith, and Diane Adreon. *Asperger Syndrome and Adolescence: Practical Solutions for School Success.* Shawnee Mission, KS: Autism Asperger Publishing Company, 2001.

Myles, Haley Morgan. *Practical Solutions to Everyday Challenges for Children with Asperger Syndrome.* Shawnee Mission, KS: Autism Asperger Publishing Company, 2002.

Ozonoff, Sally, Geraldine Dawson, and James McPartland. *A Parent's Guide to Asperger Syndrome and High-Functioning Autism.* New York: Guilford Press, 2002.

Bibliography

Attwood, Tony, and Lorna Wing. *Asperger's Syndrome: A Guide for Parents and Professionals.* London: Jessica Kingsly Publishers, 1998.

Baron-Cohen, Simon. *Mindblindness: An Essay on Autism and Theory of Mind.* Cambridge, MA: MIT Press, 1995.

Bashe, Patricia Romanowski, Barbara L. Kirby, and Tony Attwood. *The OASIS Guide to Asperger Syndrome: Advice, Support, Insight, and Inspiration.* New York: Crown Publishing, 2001.

Frith, Uta. *Autism: Explaining the Enigma.* Oxford, England: Blackwell Publishers, 1989.

Grandin, Temple. *Thinking in Pictures: And Other Reports from My Life with Autism.* New York: Vintage Books, 1996.

Hewetson, Ann. *The Stolen Child: Aspects of Autism and Asperger Syndrome.* Westport, CT: Bergin & Garvey, 2002.

Ozonoff, Sally, Geraldine Dawson, and James McPartland. *A Parent's Guide to Asperger Syndrome and High-Functioning Autism.* New York: Guilford Press, 2002.

Powers, Michael, and Janet Poland. *Asperger Syndrome and Your Child: A Parent's Guide.* New York: HarperResource, 2002.

Waltz, Mitzi. *Autistic Spectrum Disorders: Understanding the Diagnosis and Getting Help.* Sebastopol, CA: Patient-Centered Guides, 2002.

Source Notes

Chapter 1

1. Michael Powers and Janet Poland, *Asperger Syndrome and Your Child: A Parent's Guide* (New York: HarperResource, 2002), p. 12.
2. Dr. Richard Howlin, "Understanding Asperger Syndrome." Retrieved December 13, 2002 (http://www.kandi.org/aspergers/Detailed/106.html).
3. *ASPEN*, Articles by persons with Asperger syndrome. Retrieved December 12, 2002 (http://www.aspennj.org).
4. Author interview with Barbara Oxenfeldt, March 2003.
5. Author interview with Dr. Raun Melmed, March 2003.
6. Ibid.
7. Author interview with Dr. Brenda Smith Myles, March 2003.
8. Author interview with Adam Shery, March 2003.
9. Author interview with Dr. Steven Wolf, March 2003.

Chapter 2

1. Author interview with Dr. Raun Melmed, March 2003.
2. Dr. Stephen Bauer, "Asperger Syndrome," Online Asperger Syndrome Information and Support. Retrieved December 13, 2002 (http://www.udel.edu/bkirby/asperger).
3. Ami Klin and Fred R. Volkmar, "Review of Asperger Syndrome." Retrieved December 17, 2002 (http://info.med.yale.edu/chldstdy/autism).
4. Melmed Center. Retrieved February 25, 2003 (http://www.melmedcenter.com).
5. Author interview with Dr. Brenda Smith Myles, March 2003.
6. Author interview with Dr. Jed Baker, March 2003.

Chapter 3

1. Michael Powers and Janet Poland, *Asperger Syndrome and Your Child: A Parent's Guide* (New York: HarperResource, 2002), p. 19.
2. Author interview with Helene Lesser, March 2003.
3. Author interview with anonymous source, March 2003.
4. Cara Nissman, "Facing Asperger Syndrome," *Boston Herald*, November 10, 2002.
5. Author interview with Lori Shery, March 2003.
6. Author interview with Dr. Norma Doft, March 2003.
7. Author interview with Dr. Elizabeth Roberts, March 2003.
8. Powers and Poland, p. 19.

Chapter 5

1. Uta Frith, *Autism: Explaining the Enigma* (Oxford, England: Blackwell Publishers, 2003), pp. 19–24.

Chapter 6

1. Oliver Sacks, *An Anthropologist on Mars: Seven Paradoxical Tales* (New York: Random House, 1995), p. 258.
2. *ASPEN*, Articles by persons with Asperger syndrome. Retrieved December 13, 2002 (http://www.aspennj.org).
3. Cindy Little, "Which Is It? AS or Giftedness?" *Gifted Child Today*, Winter 2002, p. 30.
4. *ASPEN*.
5. Nicholas Barrow, "The Bounds of Reasonable Behavior," *The Spectator*, September 28, 2002.
6. "He's Not an Oddball, He's Just Different," *The Straits Times*, November 24, 2002.

7. Marc Segar, "A Survival Guide for People with AS." Retrieved December 13, 2002 (http://www.shifth .mistral.co.uk/autism/marc1.htm).
8. Author interview with Joan Harrington, February 3, 2003.
9. Author interview with Dr. Brenda Smith Myles, March 2003.
10. Author interview with Ronee Groff, December 2001.
11. Author interview with Dr. Vicki Sudhalter, March 2003.
12. Author interview with Dr. Raun Melmed, March 2003.
13. Author interview with anonymous source, March 2, 2003.
14. Geoffrey Cowley, "Understanding Autism," *Newsweek*, July 31, 2000.
15. Author interview with Mary Clancy, March 2003.
16. Author interview with Barbara Oxenfeldt, March 2003.

Chapter 7
1. Ann Hewetson, *The Stolen Child: Aspects of Autism and Asperger Syndrome* (Westport, CT: Bergin & Garvey, 2002), p. 45.
2. Author interview with Vivian Polo, January 2003.
3. Author interview with Dr. Bridget Taylor, March 2003.
4. Author interview with Dr. Jed Baker, March 2003.
5. Author interview with Dr. Brenda Smith Myles, March 2003.

6. Author interview with Dr. Bridget Taylor.
7. "Book Is Road Map to Help Parents Find Their Child," Ascribe Newswire. Retrieved July 16, 2002 (http://web.lexis-nexis.com/universe/document).
8. Author interview with Barbara Oxenfeldt, March 2003.
9. Sally Ozonoff, Geraldine Dawson, and James McPartland. *A Parent's Guide to Asperger Syndrome and High-Functioning Autism* (New York: Guilford Press, 2002), p. 115.
10. Michael Powers and Janet Poland, *Asperger Syndrome and Your Child: A Parent's Guide* (New York: HarperResource, 2002), pp. 183–184.
11. Author interview with Lori Shery, December 12, 2002.
12. Stephen Bauer, "Asperger Syndrome," Online Asperger Syndrome Information and Support. Retrieved December 13, 2002 (http://www.udel.edu/bkirby/asperger).
13. Lynette M. Henderson. "AS in Gifted Individuals," *Gifted Children Today*, Summer 2001.

Chapter 8
1. Author interview with Lori Shery, March 2003.
2. "Book Is Road Map to Help Parents Find Their Child," Ascribe Newswire. Retrieved July 16, 2002 (http://web.lexis-nexis.com/universe/document).
3. Author interview with anonymous source, June 28, 1999.
4. Sally Ozonoff, Geraldine Dawson, and James McPartland. *A Parent's Guide to Asperger Syndrome and High-Functioning Autism* (New York: Guilford Press, 2002), p. 75.

5. Author interview with Dr. Raun Melmed, March 2003.
6. Linda Lamb, interview with Mitzi Waltz. Retrieved January 24, 2003 (http://www.patientcenters.com).
7. Author interview with Margaret Benjamin, July 3, 2003.

Index

About the Author

Maxine Rosaler is the mother of an eleven-year-old boy with Asperger syndrome.

Editor: Nicholas Croce; Layout: Tom Forget